TRANSFORMERS

VOLUME 2: TRANSPORT TO OBLIVION

DANIEL WARREN JOHNSON
WRITER

JORGE CORONA
ARTIST

MIKE SPICER
COLORIST

RUS WOOTON
LETTERER

DANIEL WARREN JOHNSON & MIKE SPICER
KEI ZAMA
DAVID MACK
COVERS

BEN ABERNATHY
EDITOR

ANDRES JUAREZ
PUBLICATION DESIGN

RICHARD MERCADO
PRODUCTION

SPECIAL THANKS TO HASBRO'S ED LANE, MICHAEL COHN, LINDA LEE & TAYLA REO FOR THEIR INVALUABLE ASSISTANCE.

Licensed by:

FOR SKYBOUND ENTERTAINMENT:

FOR SKYBOUND ENTERTAINMENT: ROBERT KIRKMAN *CHAIRMAN* | **DAVID ALPERT** *CEO* | **SEAN MACKIEWICZ** *SVP, PUBLISHER* | **ANDRES JUAREZ** *CREATIVE DIRECTOR, EDITORIAL* | **ARUNE SINGH** *VP, BRAND, EDITORIAL* | **SHANNON MEEHAN** *SENIOR PUBLIC RELATIONS MANAGER* | **ALEX ANTONE** *EDITORIAL DIRECTOR* | **BEN ABERNATHY** *EXECUTIVE EDITOR* | **NACHIE MARSHAM** *SENIOR EDITOR* | **BLAKE KOBASHIGAWA** *SENIOR DIRECTOR, BUSINESS DEVELOPMENT, EDITORIAL* | **JILLIAN CRAB** *GRAPHIC DESIGNER* | **ASHBY FLORENCE** *PRODUCTION ARTIST* | **RICHARD MERCADO** *PRODUCTION ARTIST* | **ALEX HARGETT** *DIRECTOR OF BRAND, EDITORIAL* | **SARAH CLEMENTS** *BRAND COORDINATOR, EDITORIAL* | **ANNA GEORGE** *BRAND COORDINATOR, EDITORIAL* | **GREG FOREMAN** *SENIOR CROWDFUNDING MANAGER* | **DAN PETERSEN** *SENIOR DIRECTOR, OPERATIONS & EVENTS* | Foreign Rights & Licensing Inquiries: foreignlicensing@skybound.com | **SKYBOUND.COM**

FOR IMAGE COMICS, INC:

FOR IMAGE COMICS, INC: ROBERT KIRKMAN *CHIEF OPERATING OFFICER* | **ERIK LARSEN** *CHIEF FINANCIAL OFFICER* | **TODD MCFARLANE** *PRESIDENT* | **MARC SILVESTRI** *CHIEF EXECUTIVE OFFICER* | **JIM VALENTINO** *EXECUTIVE VICE PRESIDENT* | **ERIC STEPHENSON** *PUBLISHER / CHIEF CREATIVE OFFICER* | **NICOLE LAPALME** *VICE PRESIDENT OF FINANCE* | **LEANNA CAUNTER** *ACCOUNTING ANALYST* | **SUE KORPELA** *ACCOUNTING & HR MANAGER* | **ALEX COX** *DIRECTOR OF DIRECT MARKET SALES* | **MARGOT WOOD** *VICE PRESIDENT OF BOOK MARKET SALES* | **CHLOE RAMOS** *BOOK MARKET & LIBRARY SALES MANAGER* | **KAT SALAZAR** *VICE PRESIDENT OF PR & MARKETING* | **DEANNA PHELPS** *MARKETING DESIGN MANAGER* | **JIM VISCARDI** *VICE PRESIDENT OF BUSINESS DEVELOPMENT* | **LORELEI BUNJES** *VICE PRESIDENT OF DIGITAL STRATEGY* | **EMILIO BAUTISTA** *DIGITAL SALES COORDINATOR* | **DIRK WOOD** *VICE PRESIDENT OF INTERNATIONAL SALES & LICENSING* | **RYAN BREWER** *INTERNATIONAL SALES & LICENSING MANAGER* | **DREW GILL** *ART DIRECTOR* | **HEATHER DOORNINK** *VICE PRESIDENT OF PRODUCTION* | **IAN BALDESSARI** *PRINT MANAGER* | **MELISSA GIFFORD** *CONTENT MANAGER* | **DREW FITZGERALD** *CONTENT MANAGER* | **FRTKA SCHNATZ** *SFNIOR PRODUCTION ARTIST* | **WESLEY GRIFFITH** *PRODUCTION ARTIST* | **RICH FOWLKS** *PRODUCTION ARTIST* | **JON SCHLAFFMAN** *PRODUCTION ARTIST* | **IMAGECOMICS.COM**

TRANSFORMERS VOLUME 2. FIRST PRINTING.
ISBN: 978-1-5343-4527-0
DM ISBN: 978-1-5343-5486-9
VERSE COMICS ISBN: 978-1-5343-2672-9
TOP SHELF ISBN: 978-1-5343-2677-4

PUBLISHED BY IMAGE COMICS, INC. OFFICE OF PUBLICATION:PO BOX 14457, PORTLAND, OR 97293. ORIGINALLY PUBLISHED IN SINGLE MAGAZINE FORMAT AS TRANSFORMERS #7-12. PRINTED IN CANADA

VOLUME 02

/BEGIN/

CYBERTRON.
HURRY! THIS WAY!
THEY'RE CLOSING IN! WE'VE GOTTA MOVE!
AMBUSH!
HOW DID THEY KNOW WHERE WE--?
KEEP YOUR MIND ON THE MISSION, HUFFER!
HE'S IN THAT FORTRESS! THAT'S WHERE WE GO!
THAT'S A LONG WAY WITH NO COVER, ELITA.
WE'RE COMPLETELY CUT OFF, KUP. THE ONLY WAY OUT IS THROUGH. WE MAKE A RUN FOR IT FROM HERE.
YOU'RE SURE ABOUT THIS?
NO CHOICE. AND DON'T ASK ME AGAIN.
YOU'RE THE BOSS. HUFFER! WARPATH! LOAD UP!
READY, SARGE.
HUFFER, HOW MUCH JUICE YOU GOT?
SHIELD CAPACITY IS AT SEVEN PERCENT. I'M NOT SURE HOW MUCH LONGER IT WILL HOLD.
YOU COVER OUR REAR AS WE MAKE A RUN FOR IT.
GONNA HAVE TO HAUL ASS.
WHAT ELSE IS NEW?

PEEW
PEEW
PEEW
LET'S GO!
HERE IT COMES!
GET BEHIND ME!
ZWOK
ZWOK
OH NO, I'M **LOSING** IT--
HUKKK!
ZHKROOMM
HUFFER!!!
KEEP GOING! WE'RE ALMOST THERE!!!

ZAKK ZAKK
ZAKK
SPARKDAMNED DECEPTI-- AGH!
KUP!!!
ZAKK ZAKK
ZAKK
AIEEE!!!
FOOM
GO!
SAVE HIM!
FOR ALL OF U--!
BAM
...HELLO?
BY THE SPARK--

WHAT...
WHAT HAVE THEY DONE TO YOU?

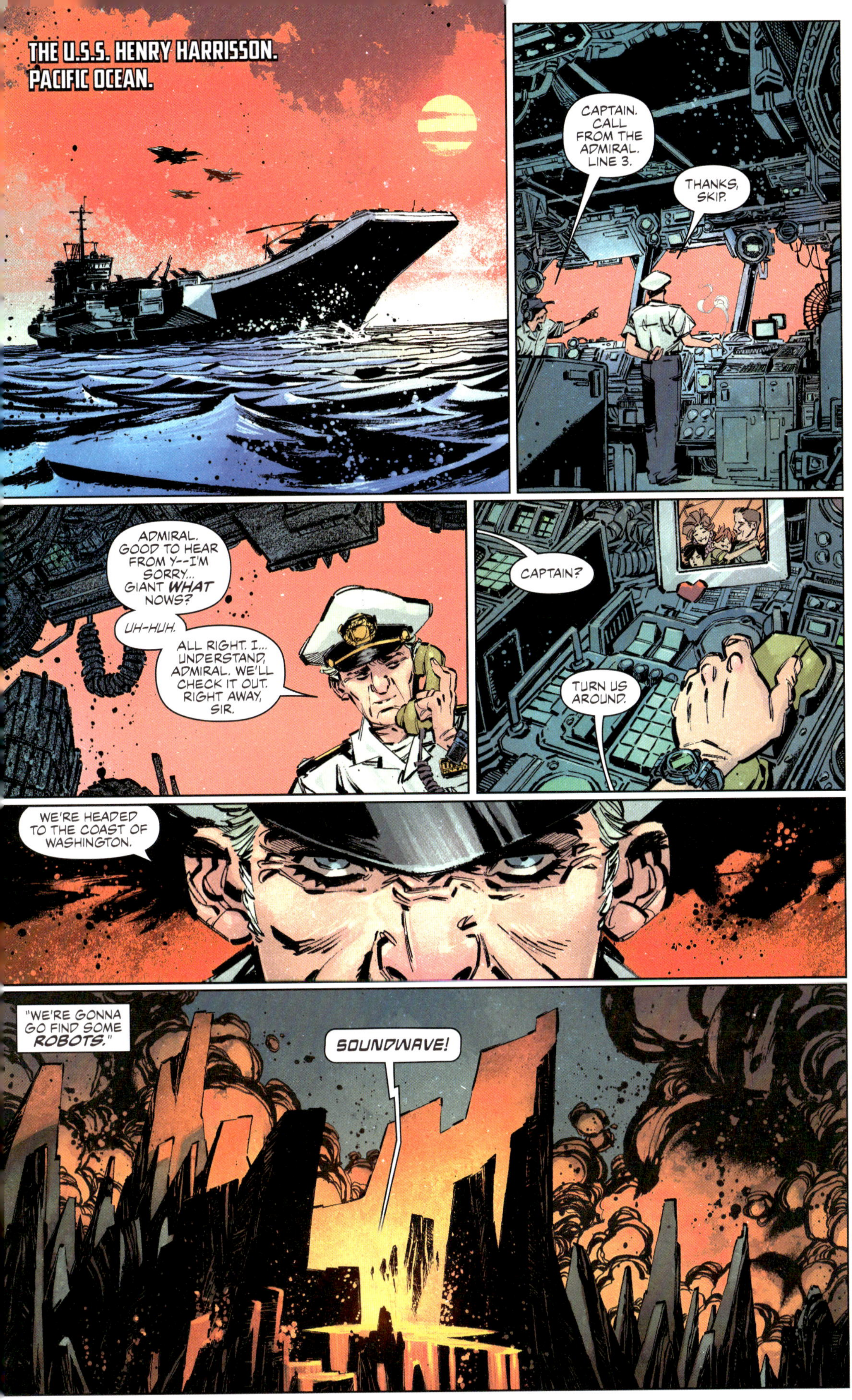
THE U.S.S. HENRY HARRISSON. PACIFIC OCEAN.
CAPTAIN. CALL FROM THE ADMIRAL. LINE 3.
THANKS, SKIP.
ADMIRAL. GOOD TO HEAR FROM Y--I'M SORRY... GIANT WHAT NOWS?
UH-HUH.
ALL RIGHT. I... UNDERSTAND, ADMIRAL. WE'LL CHECK IT OUT. RIGHT AWAY, SIR.
CAPTAIN?
TURN US AROUND.
WE'RE HEADED TO THE COAST OF WASHINGTON.
"WE'RE GONNA GO FIND SOME ROBOTS."
SOUNDWAVE!

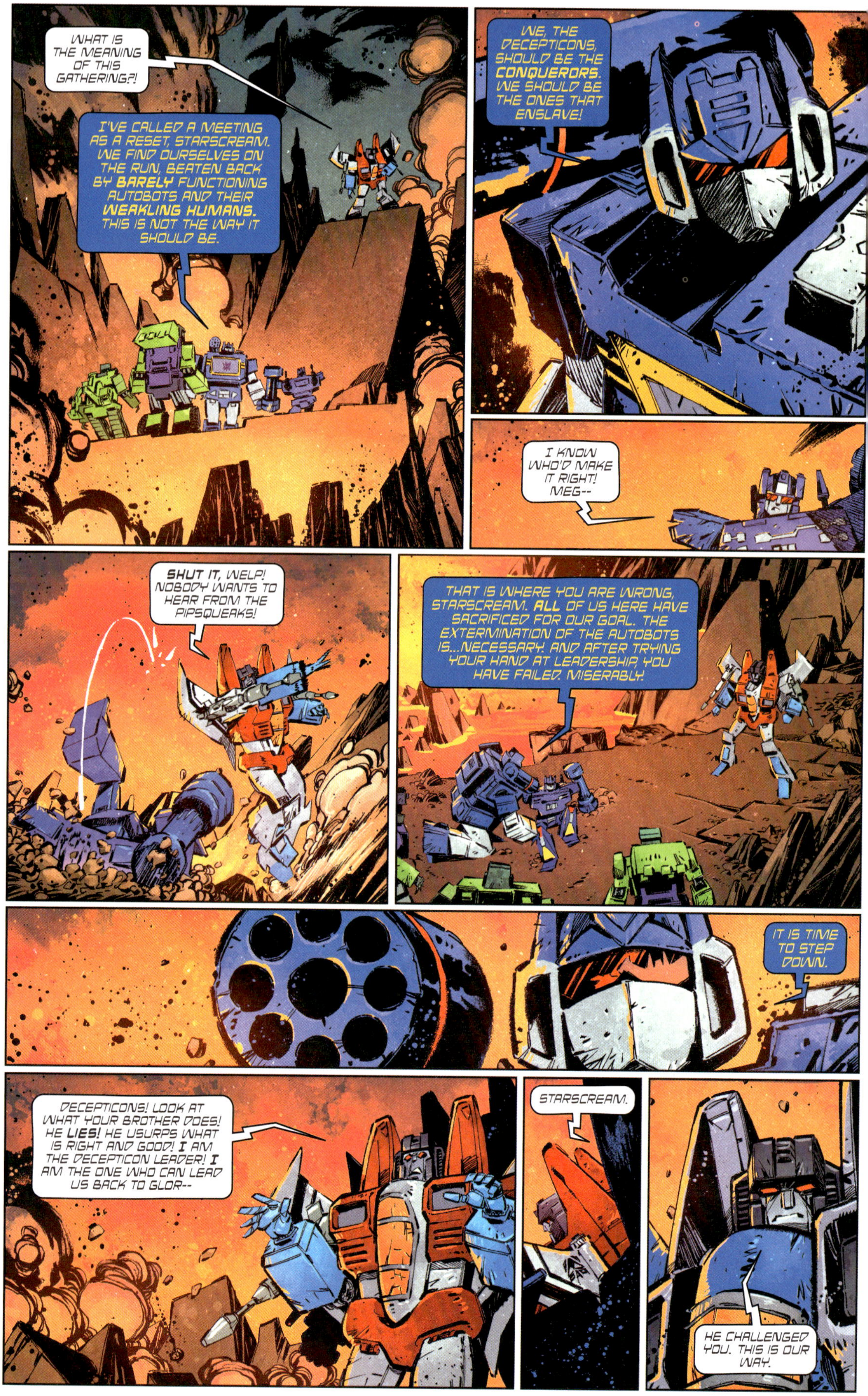
WHAT IS THE MEANING OF THIS GATHERING?!
I'VE CALLED A MEETING AS A RESET, STARSCREAM. WE FIND OURSELVES ON THE RUN, BEATEN BACK BY **BARELY** FUNCTIONING AUTOBOTS AND THEIR **WEAKLING HUMANS.** THIS IS NOT THE WAY IT SHOULD BE.
WE, THE DECEPTICONS, SHOULD BE THE **CONQUERORS.** WE SHOULD BE THE ONES THAT ENSLAVE!
I KNOW WHO'D MAKE IT RIGHT! MEG--
SHUT IT, WELP! NOBODY WANTS TO HEAR FROM THE PIPSQUEAKS!
THAT IS WHERE YOU ARE WRONG, STARSCREAM. **ALL** OF US HERE HAVE SACRIFICED FOR OUR GOAL. THE EXTERMINATION OF THE AUTOBOTS IS...NECESSARY. AND AFTER TRYING YOUR HAND AT LEADERSHIP, YOU HAVE FAILED. MISERABLY.
IT IS TIME TO STEP DOWN.
DECEPTICONS! LOOK AT WHAT YOUR BROTHER DOES! HE **LIES!** HE USURPS WHAT IS RIGHT AND GOOD! **I** AM THE DECEPTICON LEADER! **I** AM THE ONE WHO CAN LEAD US BACK TO GLOR--
STARSCREAM.
HE CHALLENGED YOU. THIS IS OUR WAY.

READY YOURSELF FOR COMBAT.
WAIT--
WAIT!!
BOOM

SOUNDWAVE-- WHAT ABOUT A CO-LEADERSHIP MOD--
THE TIME FOR TALK IS DONE.
BOOM
BOOM
FWUMP

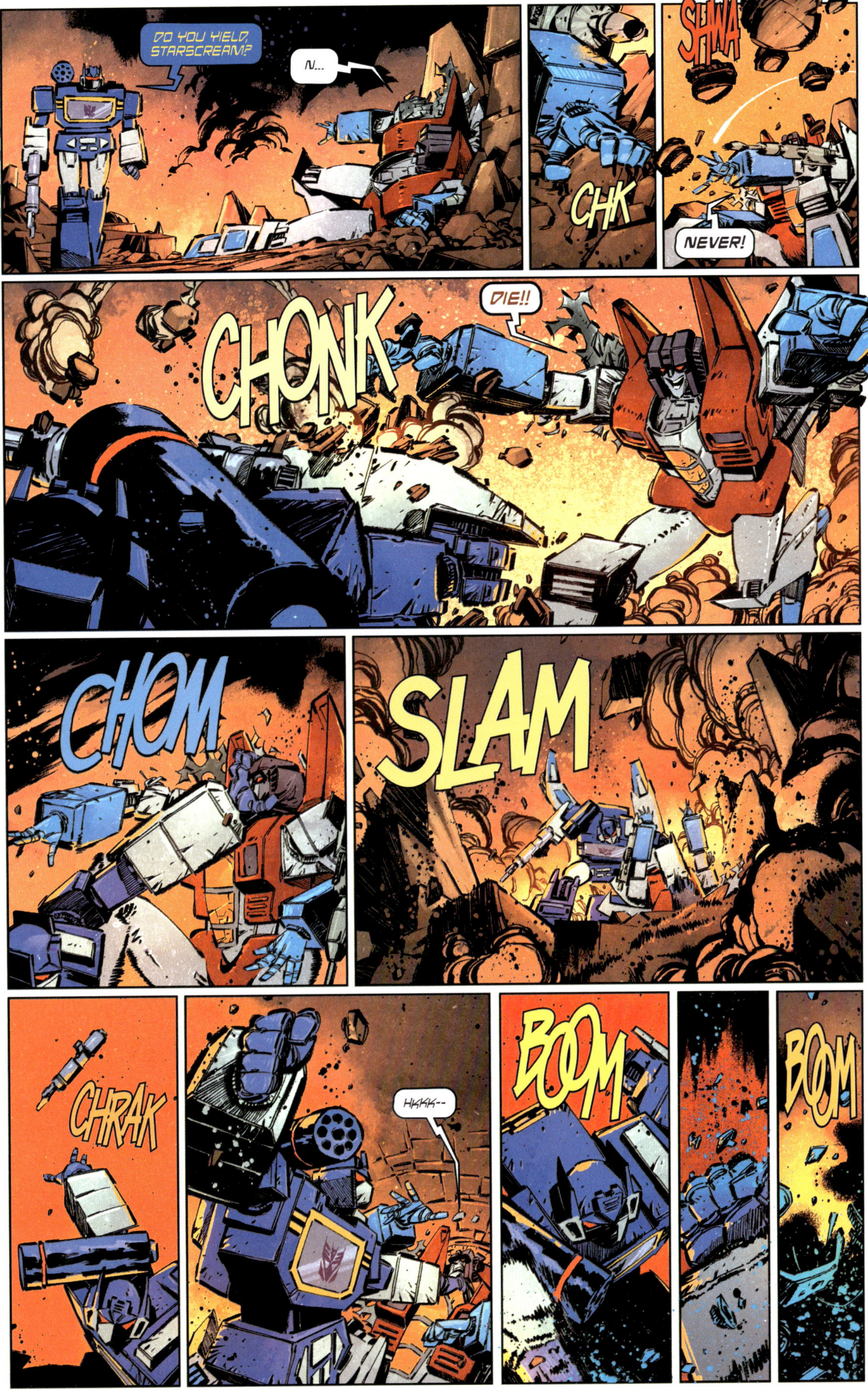
DO YOU YIELD, STARSCREAM?
N...
CHK
SHWA
NEVER!
CHONK
DIE!!
CHOM
SLAM
CHRAK
HKKK--
BOOM
BOOM

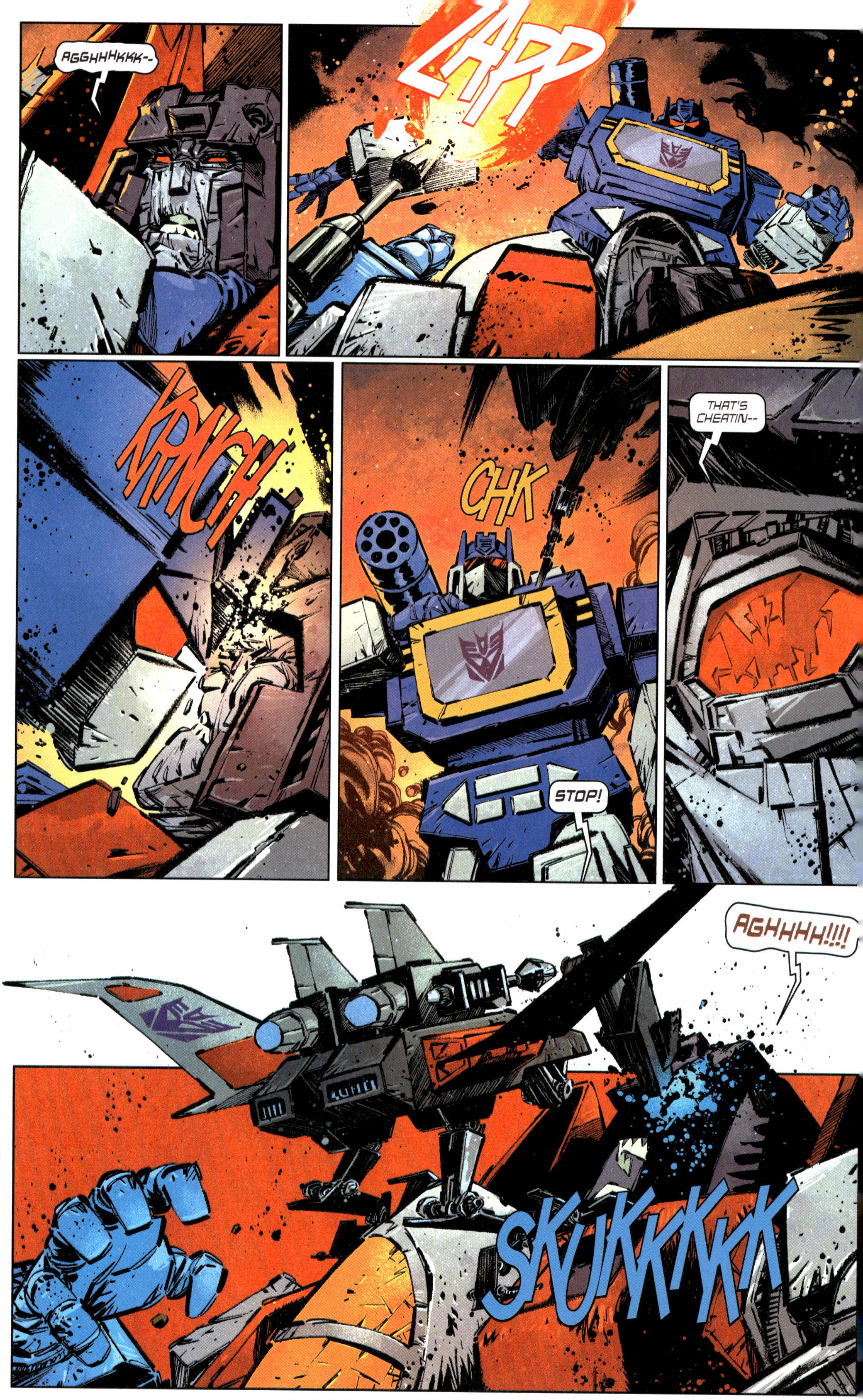
AGGHHHKKK--
ZAPP
KRNCH
CHK
STOP!
THAT'S CHEATIN--
AGHHHH!!!!
SKUKKKKK

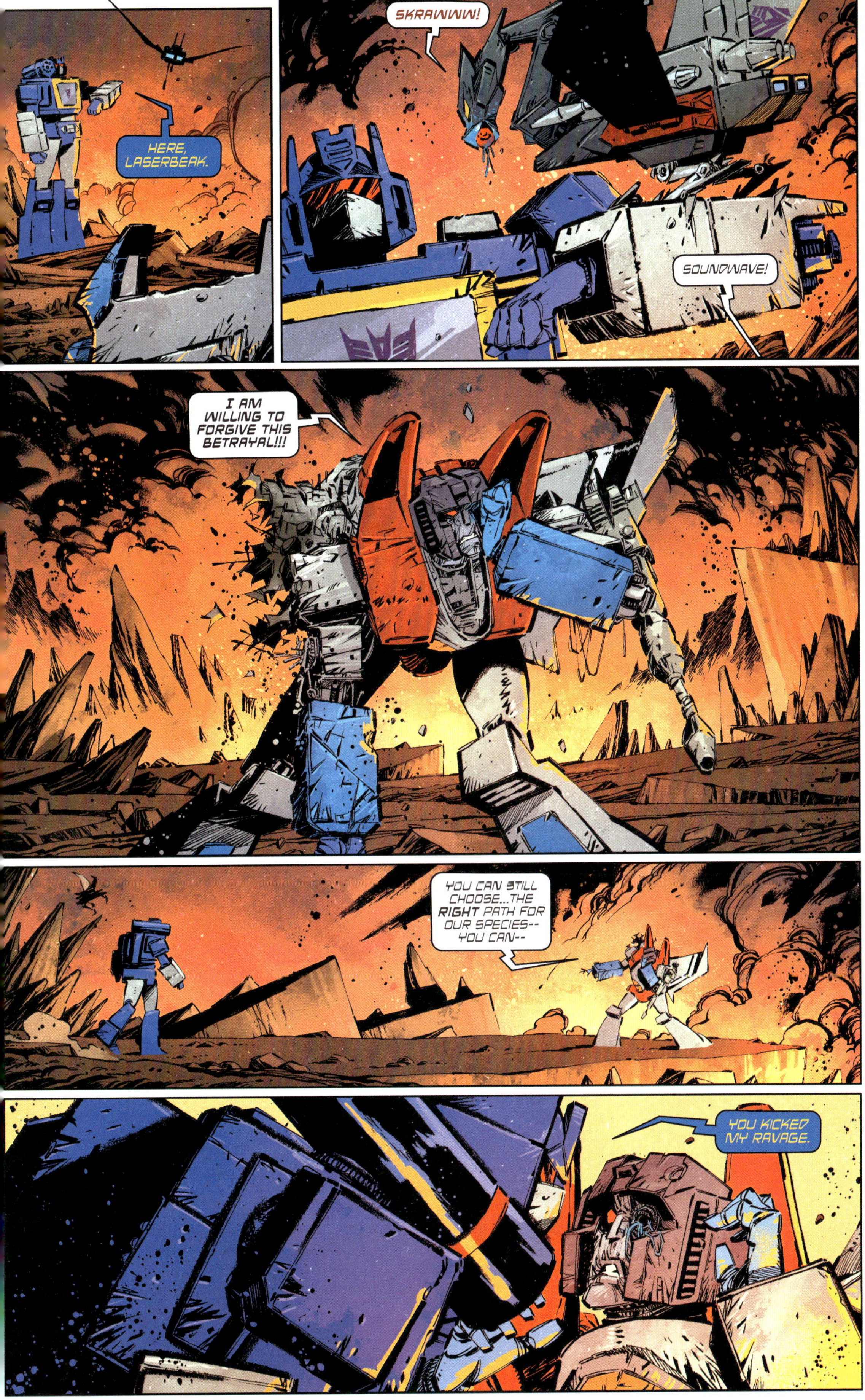
HERE, LASERBEAK.
SKRAWWW!
SOUNDWAVE!
I AM WILLING TO FORGIVE THIS BETRAYAL!!!
YOU CAN STILL CHOOSE...THE RIGHT PATH FOR OUR SPECIES-- YOU CAN--
YOU KICKED MY RAVAGE.

SHRAKK
RIPPP
THE ONLY PATH LEFT IS EXTERMINATION.
HKKK-- GHK-GK-NO--
GOODBYE, STARSCREAM.

THESE PIECES...
WILL HELP HEAL RAVAGE.
BUT I WILL NOT JUST HEAL MY OWN. WE WILL REBUILD. TOGETHER. WE WILL CONQUER. TOGETHER.
WE WILL DESTROY. TOGETHER.
ARE YOU WITH ME, BROTHERS?
CHK
CHK
CHK
CHK
DECEPTICONS! HONOR OUR NEW LEADER!
SOUNDWAVE!
SOUNDWAVE!

IT'S CARLY, ISN'T IT?
GUILTY.
WHAT ARE YOU DOING?
WHAT'S IT LOOK LIKE?
TRAINING.
IS THIS SOMETHING YOU'RE USED TO? HERE ON EARTH?
NOT REALLY.
GOTTA START SOME-WHERE.
CAN I JOIN YOU?
BOOM!!
SHOOT. SORRY.
NOT BAD.

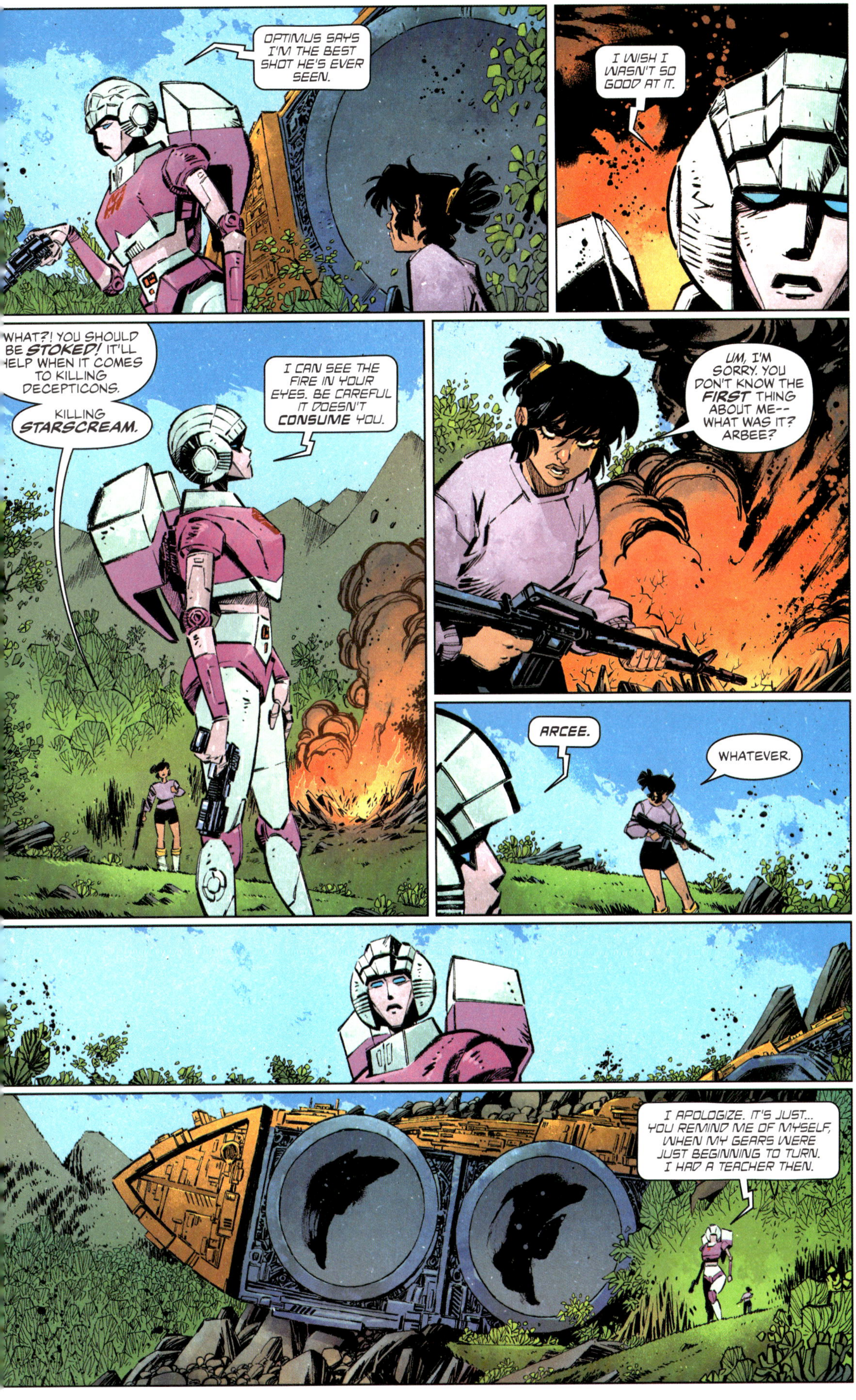
OPTIMUS SAYS I'M THE BEST SHOT HE'S EVER SEEN.
I WISH I WASN'T SO GOOD AT IT.
WHAT?! YOU SHOULD BE STOKED! IT'LL HELP WHEN IT COMES TO KILLING DECEPTICONS.
KILLING STARSCREAM.
I CAN SEE THE FIRE IN YOUR EYES. BE CAREFUL IT DOESN'T CONSUME YOU.
UM, I'M SORRY. YOU DON'T KNOW THE FIRST THING ABOUT ME-- WHAT WAS IT? ARBEE?
ARCEE.
WHATEVER.
I APOLOGIZE. IT'S JUST... YOU REMIND ME OF MYSELF, WHEN MY GEARS WERE JUST BEGINNING TO TURN. I HAD A TEACHER THEN.

"HIS NAME WAS ULTRA MAGNUS.
"MY CLAN WAS KILLED DURING THE SIEGE OF CYBERTRON WHEN I WAS VERY YOUNG. MAGNUS SAVED ME. HE WAS THE ONE THAT TAUGHT ME HOW TO SHOOT. HOW TO FIGHT.
"HE TAUGHT ME EVERYTHING I KNOW."
BUT I WANTED JUSTICE FOR MY PEOPLE. ULTRA MAGNUS DIED BECAUSE OF ME. BECAUSE OF MY PATH OF HATE. A PATH THAT TAKES MORE THAN IT HEALS, CARLY.
IF IT HEALS AT ALL.
COOL STORY.

I WAS **WEAK,** JAZZ. I COULDN'T KILL STARSCREAM.
CARLY HASN'T SPOKEN TO ME SINCE.
IT'S ALL RIGHT, CLIFF. THERE'S NO SHAME IN NOT PULLING A TRIGGER. EVEN IN WAR.
THEN WHY DO I **FEEL** THIS WAY?
IF IT MAKES IT ANY BETTER...
"OPTIMUS IS HAVING THE SAME PROBLEM."
SPIKE.
PLEASE. TALK TO ME.
I KNOW IT'S NOT YOUR FAULT, OPTIMUS.
I JUST NEED... TIME.

OPTIMUS. WHAT SPARKY DID WAS **HIS** CHOICE.
BUT...THERE'S NO WAY TO EXPLAIN THAT TO SPIKE, RATCHET. HE'S TOO YOUNG TO LOSE HIS FAMILY.
I DID THIS. I MUST MAKE IT UP TO SPIKE SOMEH-- **AGHH!**
"--WHAT--"
"OPTIMUS, WHAT'S WRONG?!
"OPTIMUS, **LOOK OUT!!!**"
SKREEEEER
KRHRUMBLLEE
WHAT HAPPENED?
I...I DON'T KNOW.
COME ON, OPTIMUS.

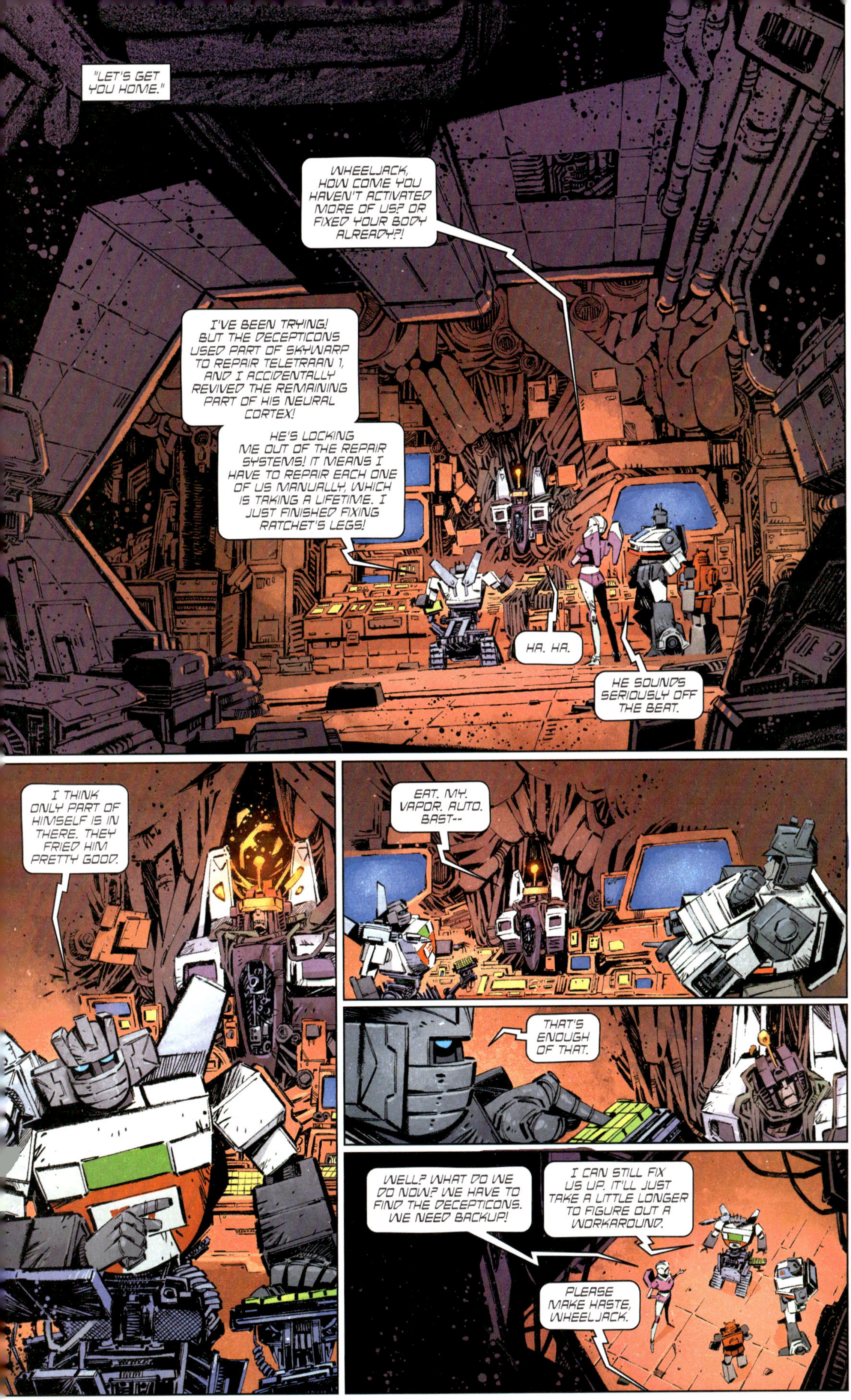
"LET'S GET YOU HOME."
WHEELJACK, HOW COME YOU HAVEN'T ACTIVATED MORE OF US? OR FIXED YOUR BODY ALREADY?!
I'VE BEEN TRYING! BUT THE DECEPTICONS USED PART OF SKYWARP TO REPAIR TELETRAAN 1, AND I ACCIDENTALLY REVIVED THE REMAINING PART OF HIS NEURAL CORTEX!
HE'S LOCKING ME OUT OF THE REPAIR SYSTEMS! IT MEANS I HAVE TO REPAIR EACH ONE OF US MANUALLY, WHICH IS TAKING A LIFETIME. I JUST FINISHED FIXING RATCHET'S LEGS!
HA. HA.
HE SOUNDS SERIOUSLY OFF THE BEAT.
I THINK ONLY PART OF HIMSELF IS IN THERE. THEY FRIED HIM PRETTY GOOD.
EAT. MY. VAPOR. AUTO. BAST--
THAT'S ENOUGH OF THAT.
WELL? WHAT DO WE DO NOW? WE HAVE TO FIND THE DECEPTICONS. WE NEED BACKUP!
I CAN STILL FIX US UP. IT'LL JUST TAKE A LITTLE LONGER TO FIGURE OUT A WORKAROUND.
PLEASE MAKE HASTE, WHEELJACK.

WE HAVE THE UPPER HAND, BUT MAKE NO MISTAKE--OUR INITIATIVE WILL NOT LAST AS LONG AS THE DECEPTICONS REIGN FREELY OVER THIS BEAUTIFUL EARTH.
IF THAT'S THE CASE, WE'LL NEED A WAY TO FIND THEM. SOME SORT OF VEHICLE TO GET US A BIRD'S-EYE VIEW.
I HAVE A PLAN FOR THAT.
STEEL YOURSELF, DECEPTICONS.
WE ARE COMING FOR YOU.

I THOUGHT THIS MIGHT BE GOOD FOR YOU. THE OPEN AIR ALWAYS CLEARS MY HEAD.
THANKS, CARLY.
HOW ARE YOU FEELING?
HONESTLY? I DON'T FEEL...ANYTHING. JUST EMPTY. THE WORLD'S CHANGED SO MUCH ALREADY.
THAT'S WHY WE HAVE TO PROTECT OURSELVES, SPIKE. AND WE'VE GOT BIG METAL WARRIORS NOW! THEY CAN HELP US GET THE ONES WHO KILLED OUR DADS!
BUT...MY DAD WASN'T KILLED. HE... GAVE HIMSELF UP FOR THEM. AND EVERY TIME I SEE THOSE ROBOTS, I CAN'T HELP BUT THINK ABOUT HOW HE JUST DISAPPEARED. NO BODY. NO ASHES. JUST GONE.
JUST LIKE JIMMY.
I DIDN'T REALIZE HOW MUCH I NEEDED HIM UNTIL HE WENT AWAY.
I DIDN'T KNOW HOW BAD IT COULD ALL GET UNTIL NOW.

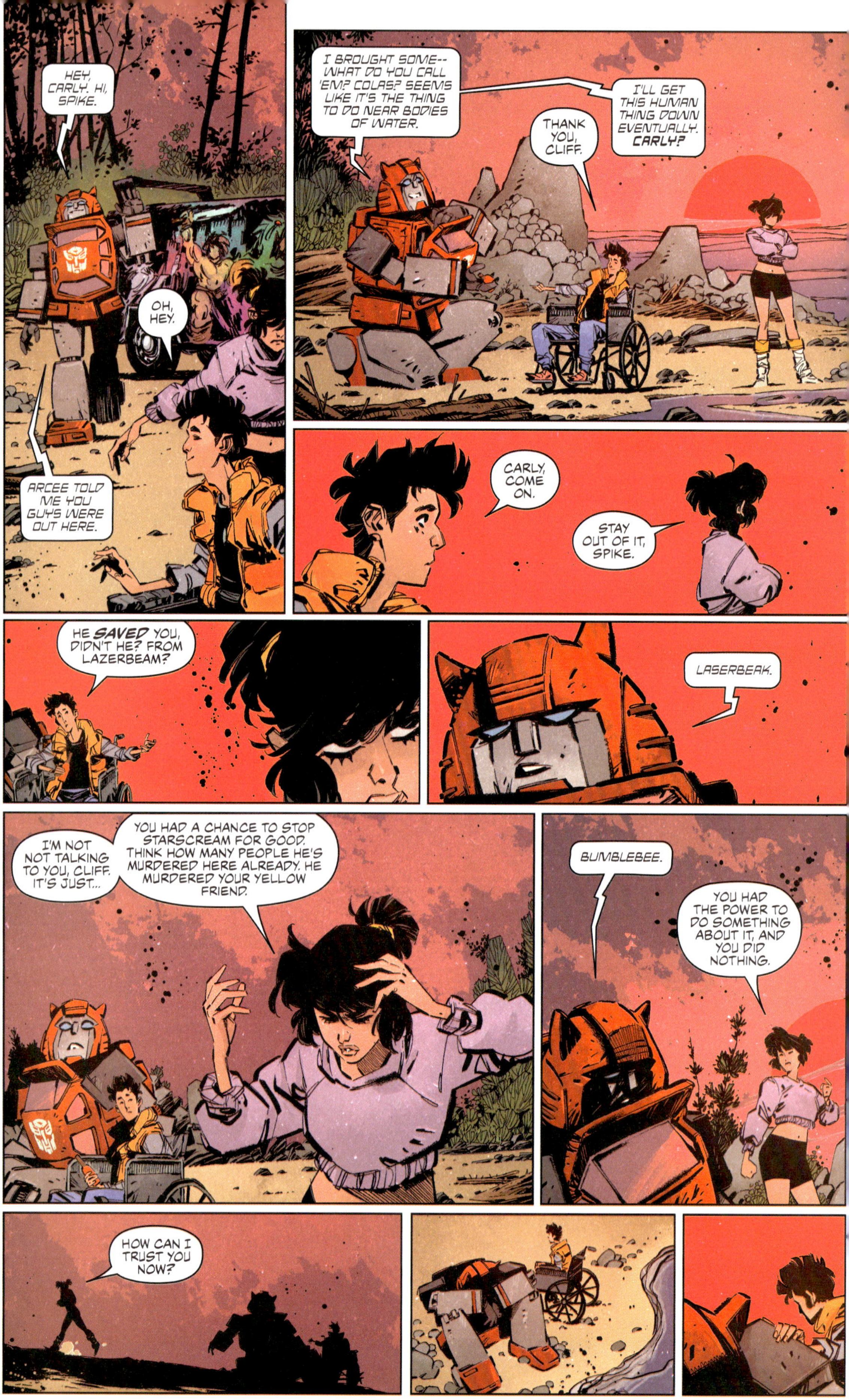
HEY, CARLY. HI, SPIKE.
ARCEE TOLD ME YOU GUYS WERE OUT HERE.
OH, HEY.
I BROUGHT SOME-- WHAT DO YOU CALL 'EM? COLAS? SEEMS LIKE IT'S THE THING TO DO NEAR BODIES OF WATER.
THANK YOU, CLIFF.
I'LL GET THIS HUMAN THING DOWN EVENTUALLY. CARLY?
CARLY, COME ON.
STAY OUT OF IT, SPIKE.
HE SAVED YOU, DIDN'T HE? FROM LAZERBEAM?
LASERBEAK.
I'M NOT NOT TALKING TO YOU, CLIFF. IT'S JUST...
YOU HAD A CHANCE TO STOP STARSCREAM FOR GOOD. THINK HOW MANY PEOPLE HE'S MURDERED HERE ALREADY. HE MURDERED YOUR YELLOW FRIEND.
BUMBLEBEE.
YOU HAD THE POWER TO DO SOMETHING ABOUT IT, AND YOU DID NOTHING.
HOW CAN I TRUST YOU NOW?

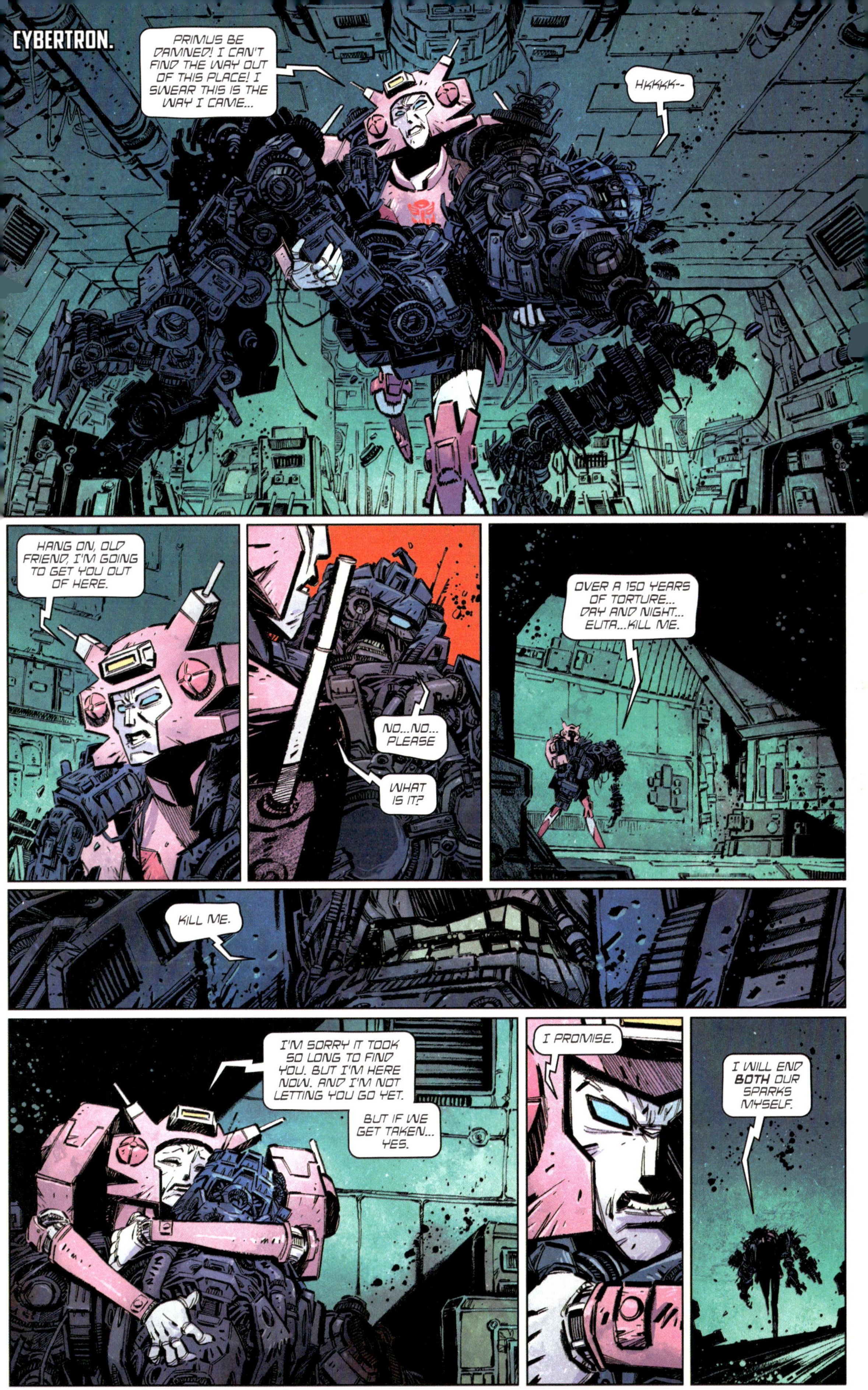

CYBERTRON.
PRIMUS BE DAMNED! I CAN'T FIND THE WAY OUT OF THIS PLACE! I SWEAR THIS IS THE WAY I CAME...
HKKKK--
HANG ON, OLD FRIEND, I'M GOING TO GET YOU OUT OF HERE.
NO...NO... PLEASE
WHAT IS IT?
OVER A 150 YEARS OF TORTURE... DAY AND NIGHT... ELITA...KILL ME.
KILL ME.
I'M SORRY IT TOOK SO LONG TO FIND YOU. BUT I'M HERE NOW. AND I'M NOT LETTING YOU GO YET.
BUT IF WE GET TAKEN... YES.
I PROMISE.
I WILL END BOTH OUR SPARKS MYSELF.

THE U.S.S. HENRY HARRISSON. PACIFIC OCEAN.
CAPTAIN! TWO UNIDENTIFIED BOGEYS COMING IN HOT, NOT RESPONDING TO OUR HAILS!
BATTLE STATIONS. GET OUR BIRDS IN THE AIR.
I'VE NEVER SEEN SOMETHING MOVE SO FAST--
AROOOO AROOOO AROOO
SKREEEEEE
VIPER 2 AND 7 LAUNCHING NOW--
THIS WHAT THEY WERE TALKING ABOUT WHEN THEY SAID "ROBOTS"?
BOGEYS CLOSING IN--
SKRAWAAAA
WHAT THE--?!
WHA- WHAT IS THAT THING?!
JUST SHOOT IT, ACOSTA!!!!
BOOM
DO NOT SINK THE SHIP YET, THUNDERCRACKER. NOT UNTIL WE ARE OVER OUR DESTINATION.

ROGER THAT, COMMANDER!
ABANDON SHIP! TO THE LIFEBOATS, HURRY!
HA! HOW STRANGE! CREATURES USING THINGS MADE OF METAL TO GET AROUND!
WHAT'S IT LIKE, HUMAN?
TO BE SO DEPENDENT ON THINGS OUTSIDE OF YOUR OWN SELF?
POW
P-PLEASE! OH GOD! I HAVE A FAMILY-- PLEASE--!

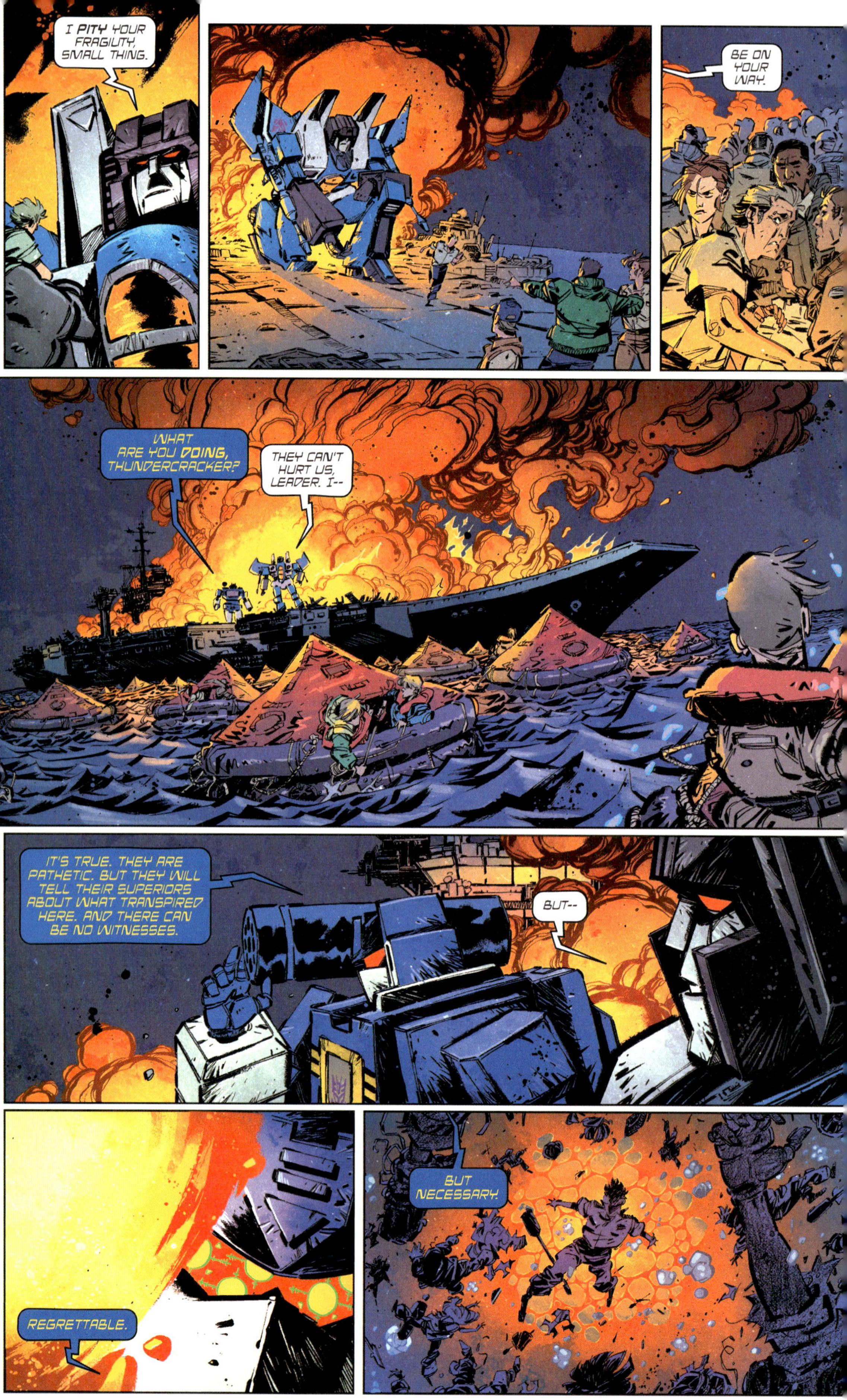
I PITY YOUR FRAGILITY, SMALL THING.
BE ON YOUR WAY.
WHAT ARE YOU DOING, THUNDERCRACKER?
THEY CAN'T HURT US, LEADER. I--
IT'S TRUE. THEY ARE PATHETIC. BUT THEY WILL TELL THEIR SUPERIORS ABOUT WHAT TRANSPIRED HERE. AND THERE CAN BE NO WITNESSES.
BUT--
REGRETTABLE.
BUT NECESSARY.

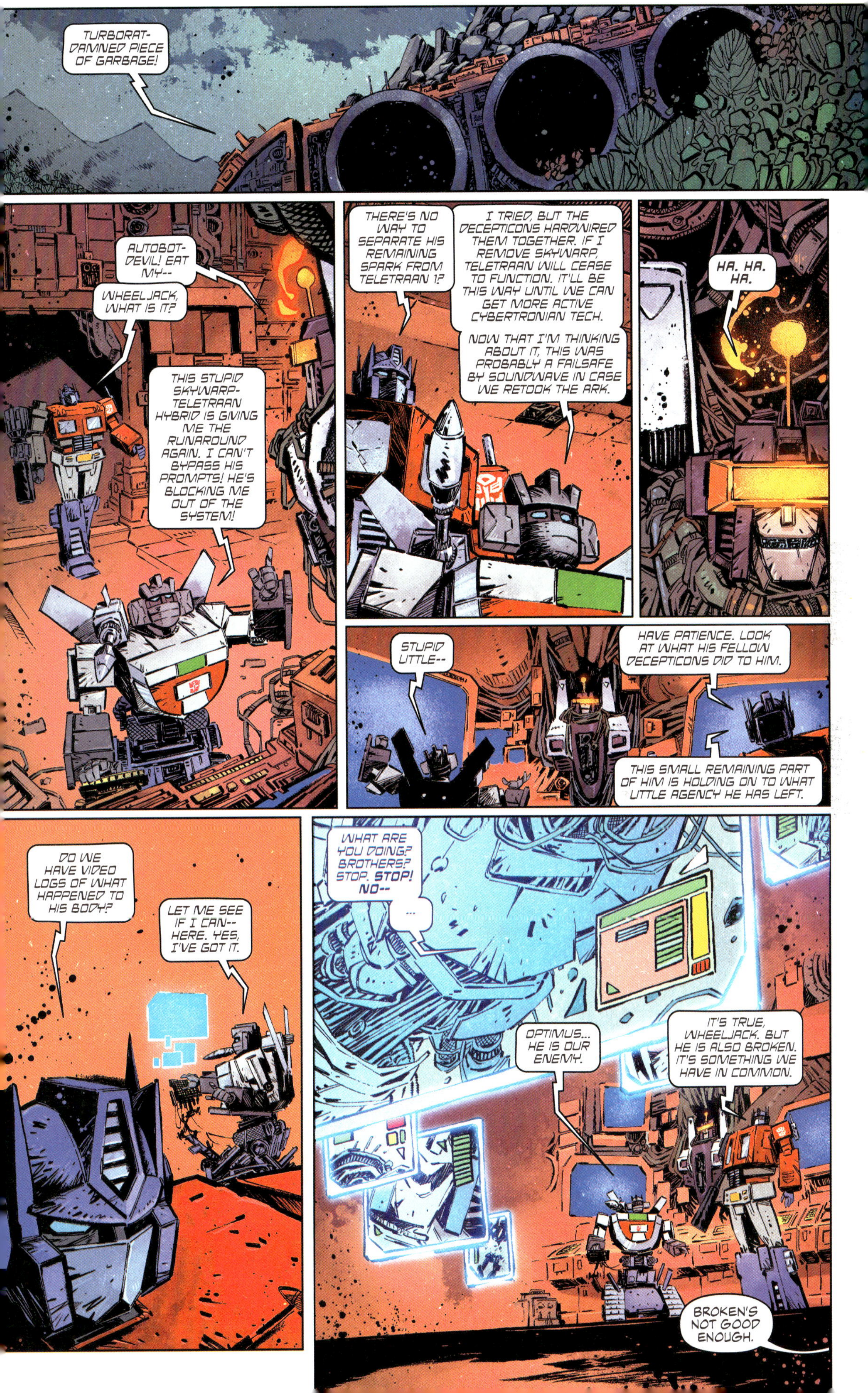
TURBORAT-DAMNED PIECE OF GARBAGE!
AUTOBOT-DEVIL! EAT MY--
WHEELJACK, WHAT IS IT?
THIS STUPID SKYWARP-TELETRAAN HYBRID IS GIVING ME THE RUNAROUND AGAIN. I CAN'T BYPASS HIS PROMPTS! HE'S BLOCKING ME OUT OF THE SYSTEM!
THERE'S NO WAY TO SEPARATE HIS REMAINING SPARK FROM TELETRAAN 1?
I TRIED, BUT THE DECEPTICONS HARDWIRED THEM TOGETHER. IF I REMOVE SKYWARP, TELETRAAN WILL CEASE TO FUNCTION. IT'LL BE THIS WAY UNTIL WE CAN GET MORE ACTIVE CYBERTRONIAN TECH.
NOW THAT I'M THINKING ABOUT IT, THIS WAS PROBABLY A FAILSAFE BY SOUNDWAVE IN CASE WE RETOOK THE ARK.
HA. HA. HA.
STUPID LITTLE--
HAVE PATIENCE. LOOK AT WHAT HIS FELLOW DECEPTICONS DID TO HIM.
THIS SMALL REMAINING PART OF HIM IS HOLDING ON TO WHAT LITTLE AGENCY HE HAS LEFT.
DO WE HAVE VIDEO LOGS OF WHAT HAPPENED TO HIS BODY?
LET ME SEE IF I CAN-- HERE. YES, I'VE GOT IT.
WHAT ARE YOU DOING? BROTHERS? STOP. STOP! NO--
...
OPTIMUS... HE IS OUR ENEMY.
IT'S TRUE, WHEELJACK. BUT HE IS ALSO BROKEN. IT'S SOMETHING WE HAVE IN COMMON.
BROKEN'S NOT GOOD ENOUGH.

DEAD IS WAY BETTER.
CHK
CARLY! PUT THE WEAPON DOWN!
WHY?! THIS ONE'S FRIENDS WITH STARSCREAM! SPIKE GOT SHOT BECAUSE OF HIM!
I KNOW. HE HAS DONE TERRIBLE THINGS. BUT WE NEED HIM TO HELP HEAL THE REST OF US. WITH THE REST OF THE AUTOBOTS, I CAN PUT AN END TO THIS WAR.
ONCE AND FOR ALL.
I--
OH, SH--!
LOOK OUT!
SHRROOAAWWW
BOOOMMMM
AGH...
ARCEE... WHY?
WHY DID YOU DO THAT?
AHA! HAHA! FINALLY!

MY LEGS! SKYWARP IS FIXING 'EM!
I KNOW IT'S HARD TO SEE, CARLY, BUT SOMETIMES WE CAN GET HELP FROM THE STRANGEST OF PL--
ARE YOU SERIOUS?! THIS IS GOING TO TURN INTO AN OPTIMUS TEACHING MOMENT?!
I--
AND WHAT AM I SUPPOSED TO DO? JUST WAIT AROUND AND GET SQUISHED?
CARLY---
NO.
I'M DONE WITH THIS.

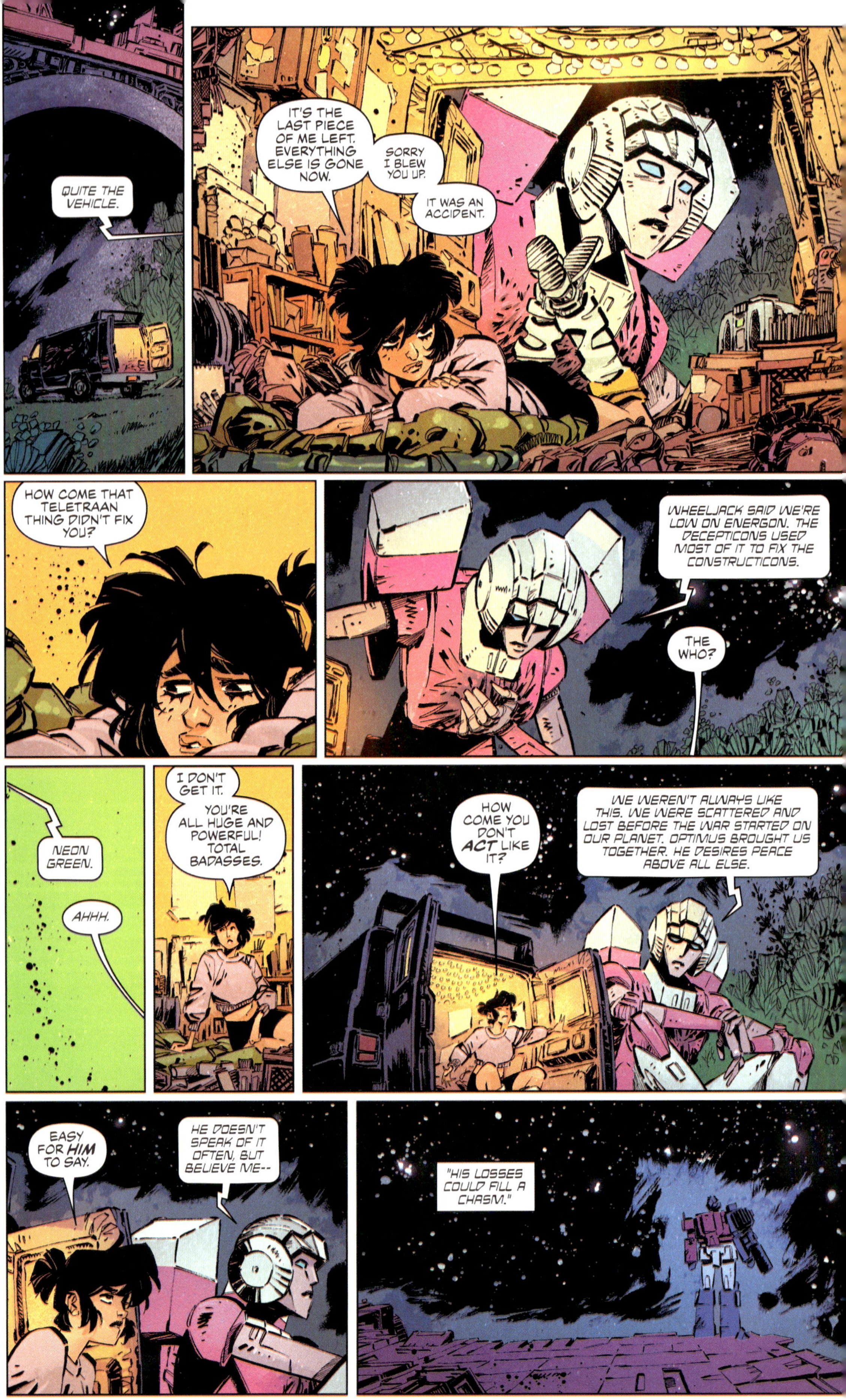
QUITE THE VEHICLE.
IT'S THE LAST PIECE OF ME LEFT. EVERYTHING ELSE IS GONE NOW.
SORRY I BLEW YOU UP.
IT WAS AN ACCIDENT.
HOW COME THAT TELETRAAN THING DIDN'T FIX YOU?
WHEELJACK SAID WE'RE LOW ON ENERGON. THE DECEPTICONS USED MOST OF IT TO FIX THE CONSTRUCTICONS.
THE WHO?
NEON GREEN.
AHHH.
I DON'T GET IT.
YOU'RE ALL HUGE AND POWERFUL! TOTAL BADASSES.
HOW COME YOU DON'T ACT LIKE IT?
WE WEREN'T ALWAYS LIKE THIS. WE WERE SCATTERED AND LOST BEFORE THE WAR STARTED ON OUR PLANET. OPTIMUS BROUGHT US TOGETHER. HE DESIRES PEACE ABOVE ALL ELSE.
EASY FOR HIM TO SAY.
HE DOESN'T SPEAK OF IT OFTEN, BUT BELIEVE ME--
"HIS LOSSES COULD FILL A CHASM."

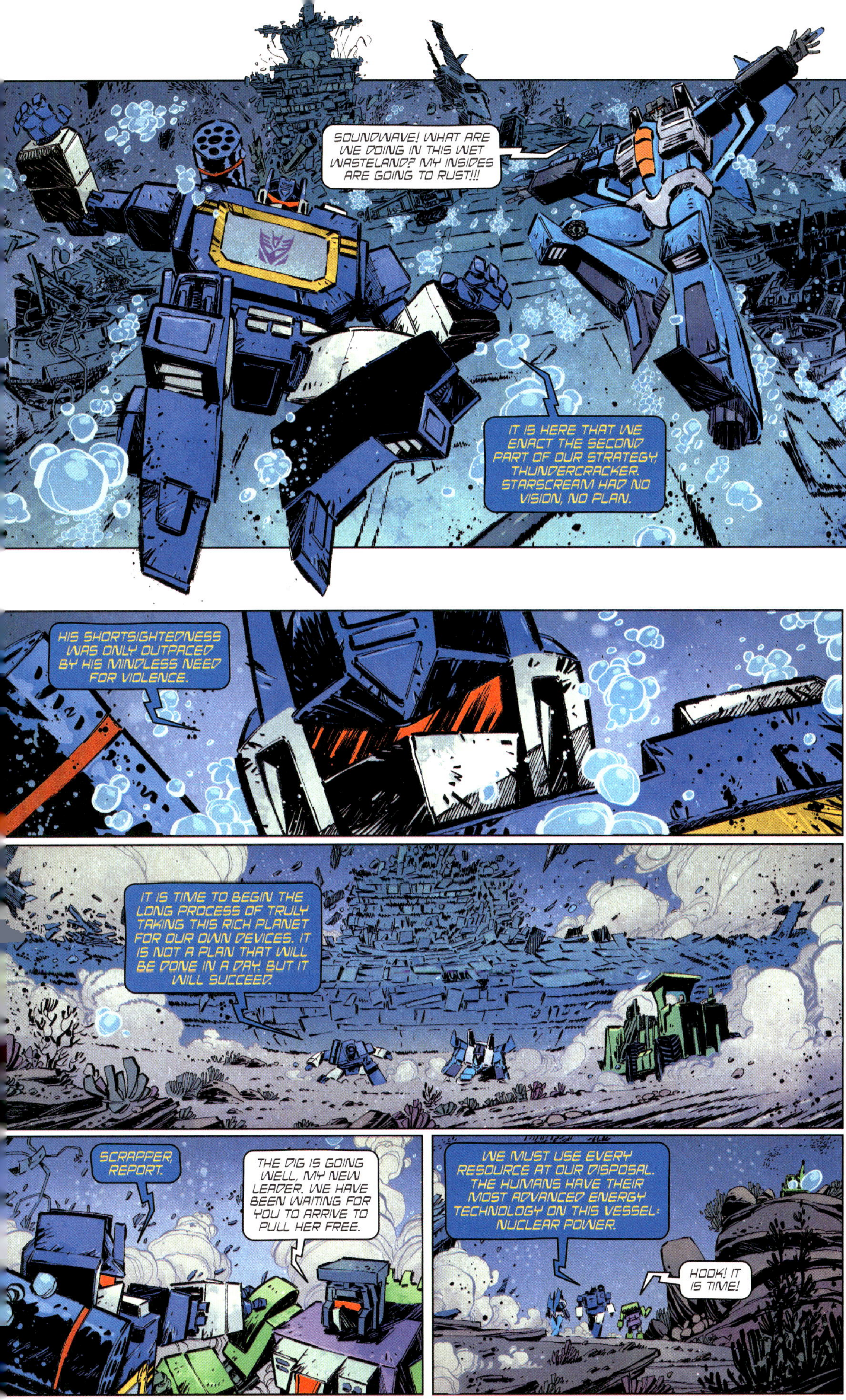
SOUNDWAVE! WHAT ARE WE DOING IN THIS WET WASTELAND?! MY INSIDES ARE GOING TO RUST!!!
IT IS HERE THAT WE ENACT THE SECOND PART OF OUR STRATEGY, THUNDERCRACKER. STARSCREAM HAD NO VISION, NO PLAN.
HIS SHORTSIGHTEDNESS WAS ONLY OUTPACED BY HIS MINDLESS NEED FOR VIOLENCE.
IT IS TIME TO BEGIN THE LONG PROCESS OF TRULY TAKING THIS RICH PLANET FOR OUR OWN DEVICES. IT IS NOT A PLAN THAT WILL BE DONE IN A DAY, BUT IT WILL SUCCEED.
SCRAPPER, REPORT.
THE DIG IS GOING WELL, MY NEW LEADER. WE HAVE BEEN WAITING FOR YOU TO ARRIVE TO PULL HER FREE.
WE MUST USE EVERY RESOURCE AT OUR DISPOSAL. THE HUMANS HAVE THEIR MOST ADVANCED ENERGY TECHNOLOGY ON THIS VESSEL: NUCLEAR POWER.
HOOK! IT IS TIME!

ROGER, COMMANDER!
WE WILL NEED IT TO AWAKEN A VESSEL OF OUR OWN.
THE NEMESIS!
INDEED.
THE VERY SHIP WE USED TO CHASE OUR ENEMIES TO THIS PLANET.

HELLO?
WHAT IS HAPPENING TO ME?
HELLO?
IS ANYONE THERE?

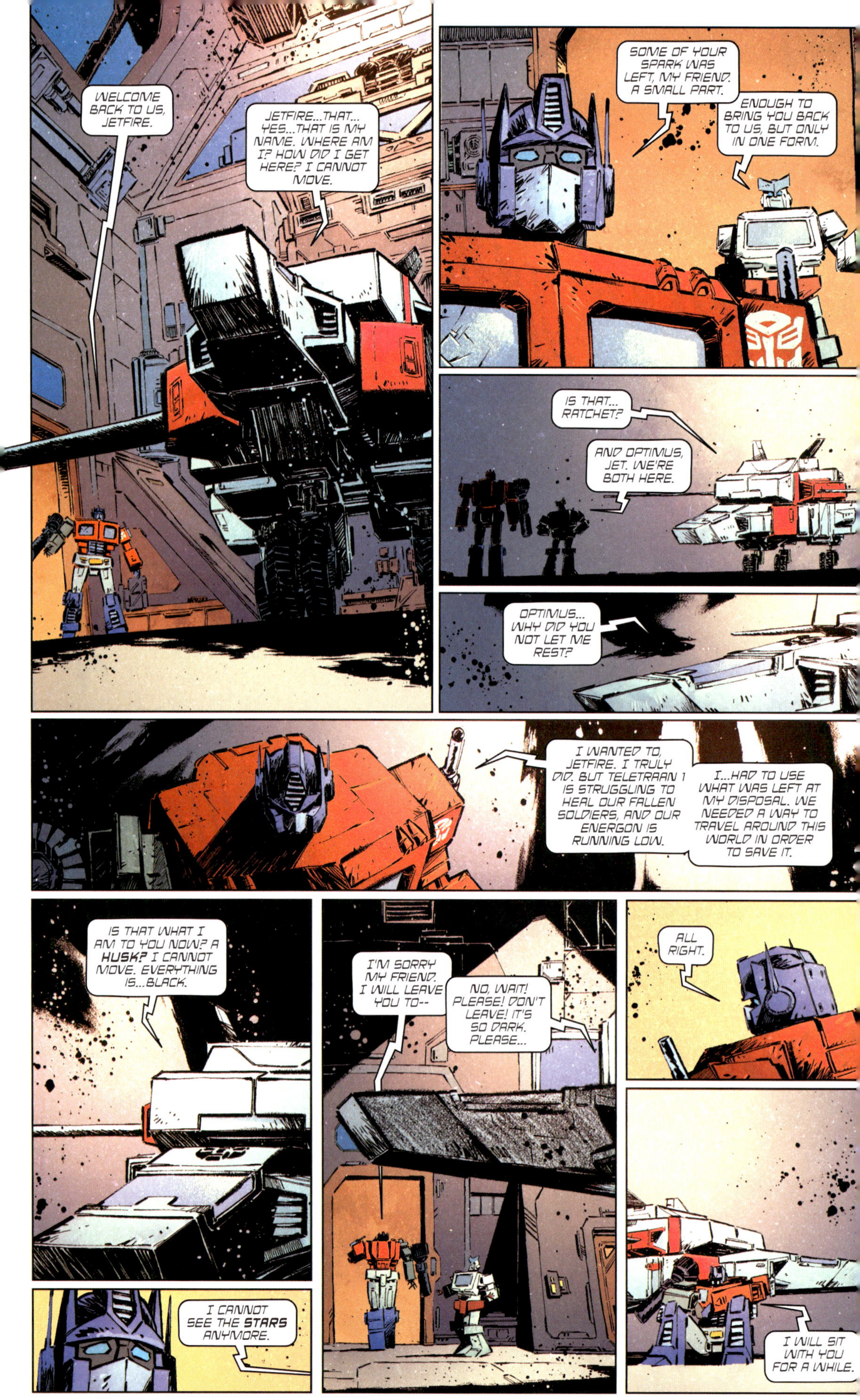
WELCOME BACK TO US, JETFIRE.
JETFIRE...THAT... YES...THAT IS MY NAME. WHERE AM I? HOW DID I GET HERE? I CANNOT MOVE.
SOME OF YOUR SPARK WAS LEFT, MY FRIEND. A SMALL PART.
ENOUGH TO BRING YOU BACK TO US, BUT ONLY IN ONE FORM.
IS THAT... RATCHET?
AND OPTIMUS, JET. WE'RE BOTH HERE.
OPTIMUS... WHY DID YOU NOT LET ME REST?
I WANTED TO, JETFIRE. I TRULY DID. BUT TELETRAAN 1 IS STRUGGLING TO HEAL OUR FALLEN SOLDIERS, AND OUR ENERGON IS RUNNING LOW.
I...HAD TO USE WHAT WAS LEFT AT MY DISPOSAL. WE NEEDED A WAY TO TRAVEL AROUND THIS WORLD IN ORDER TO SAVE IT.
IS THAT WHAT I AM TO YOU NOW? A HUSK? I CANNOT MOVE. EVERYTHING IS...BLACK.
I CANNOT SEE THE STARS ANYMORE.
I'M SORRY MY FRIEND. I WILL LEAVE YOU TO--
NO, WAIT! PLEASE! DON'T LEAVE! IT'S SO DARK. PLEASE...
ALL RIGHT.
I WILL SIT WITH YOU FOR A WHILE.

WE WILL FUNNEL THE NUCLEAR ENERGY THROUGH HERE. I HAVE BUILT A LOW LEVEL ENERGON SHIELD AROUND THE OPENING TO KEEP THE OCEAN WATER OUT.
IT'S GOOD TO BE BACK INSIDE OUR HOME AWAY FROM HOME!
BANG! BANG!
IT CAN'T BE--
YOU DON'T THINK--
WHEN THE SHIP CRASHED HERE, HE MUST HAVE ESCAPED. RIGHT?
BANG! BANG!
APPARENTLY NOT.
DO WE...?
WE NEED ALL THE HELP WE CAN GET RIGHT NOW, THUNDERCRACKER.
COMMANDER... ARE YOU SURE?
OPEN IT.
BEEP

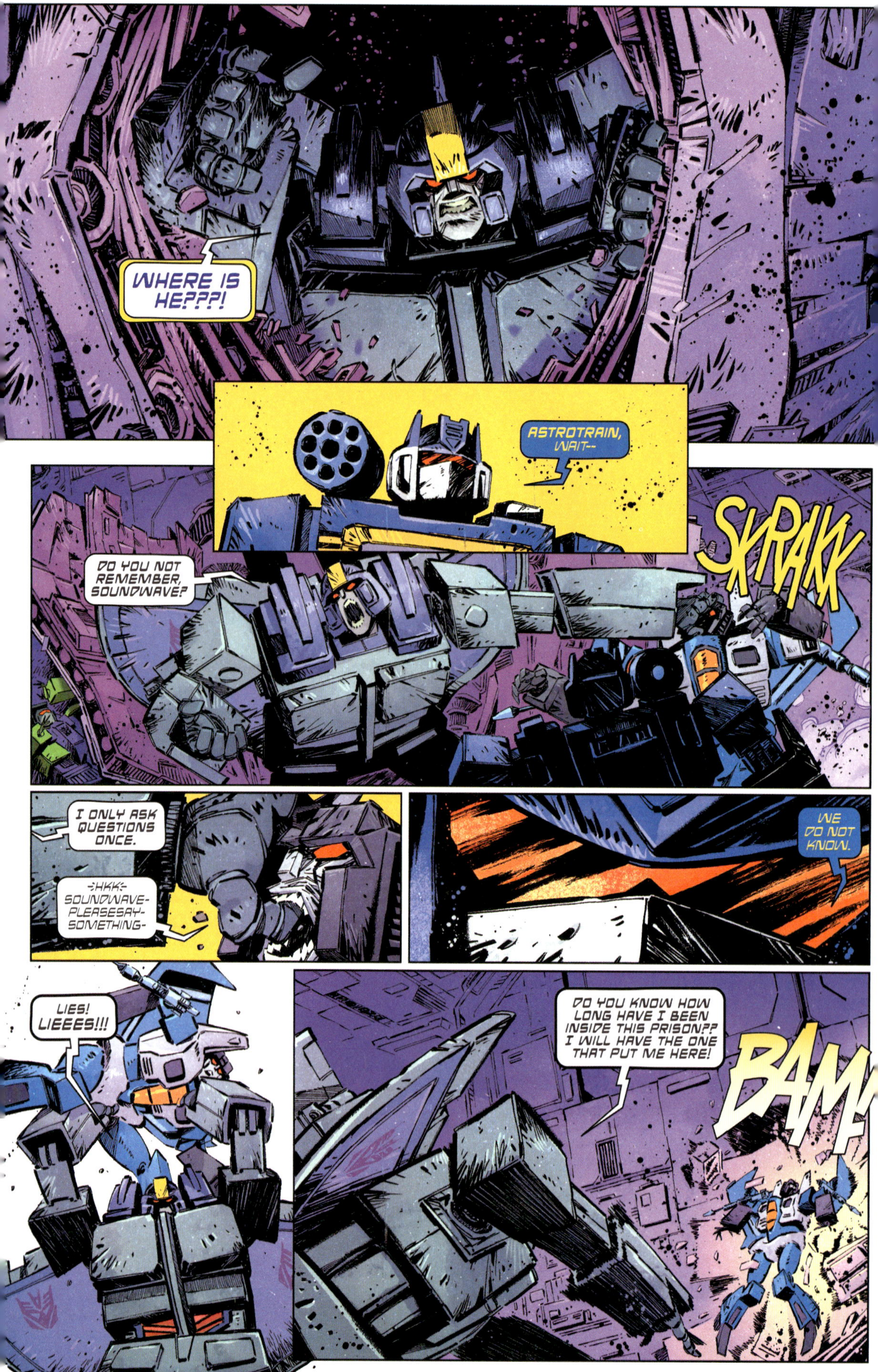
WHERE IS HE???!
ASTROTRAIN, WAIT--
SKRAKK
DO YOU NOT REMEMBER, SOUNDWAVE?
I ONLY ASK QUESTIONS ONCE.
-HKK- SOUNDWAVE-PLEASESAY-SOMETHING-
WE DO NOT KNOW.
LIES! LIEEES!!!
DO YOU KNOW HOW LONG HAVE I BEEN INSIDE THIS PRISON?? I WILL HAVE THE ONE THAT PUT ME HERE!
BAM

I WILL TEAR HIS FUEL LINES FROM THEIR TANKS! I WILL DRINK THE ENERGON FROM HIS CORE!
PLEASE-STOP--
I CANNOT GIVE YOU INFORMATION I DO NOT HAVE, WARRIOR.
SWEAR ON YOUR LIFE. AS A FIGHTER OF THE GREATER DECEPTICON GOOD.
SWEAR IT!
WHEN WE FIND HIM, I SWEAR. MEGATRON WILL BE YOURS.
TO DO WITH AS YOU WILL.
HNF.
BUT FOR NOW, I HAVE A MISSION FOR YOU.
OW.
"OPTIMUS. I'VE GOT SOMETHING."

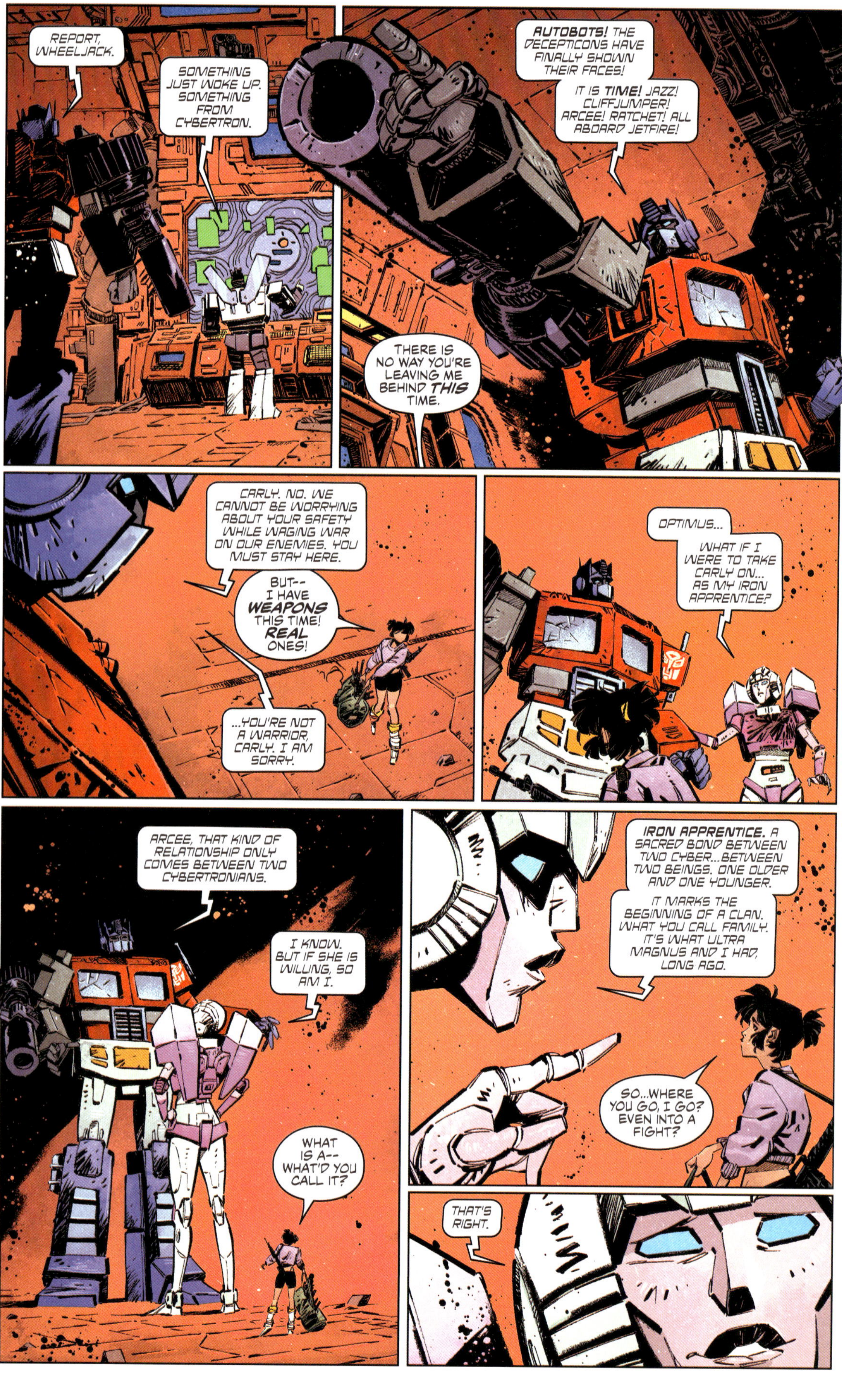
REPORT, WHEELJACK.
SOMETHING JUST WOKE UP. SOMETHING FROM CYBERTRON.
AUTOBOTS! THE DECEPTICONS HAVE FINALLY SHOWN THEIR FACES!
IT IS TIME! JAZZ! CLIFFJUMPER! ARCEE! RATCHET! ALL ABOARD JETFIRE!
THERE IS NO WAY YOU'RE LEAVING ME BEHIND THIS TIME.
CARLY. NO. WE CANNOT BE WORRYING ABOUT YOUR SAFETY WHILE WAGING WAR ON OUR ENEMIES. YOU MUST STAY HERE.
BUT-- I HAVE WEAPONS THIS TIME! REAL ONES!
...YOU'RE NOT A WARRIOR, CARLY. I AM SORRY.
OPTIMUS...
WHAT IF I WERE TO TAKE CARLY ON... AS MY IRON APPRENTICE?
ARCEE, THAT KIND OF RELATIONSHIP ONLY COMES BETWEEN TWO CYBERTRONIANS.
I KNOW. BUT IF SHE IS WILLING, SO AM I.
WHAT IS A-- WHAT'D YOU CALL IT?
IRON APPRENTICE. A SACRED BOND BETWEEN TWO CYBER...BETWEEN TWO BEINGS. ONE OLDER AND ONE YOUNGER.
IT MARKS THE BEGINNING OF A CLAN. WHAT YOU CALL FAMILY. IT'S WHAT ULTRA MAGNUS AND I HAD, LONG AGO.
SO...WHERE YOU GO, I GO? EVEN INTO A FIGHT?
THAT'S RIGHT.

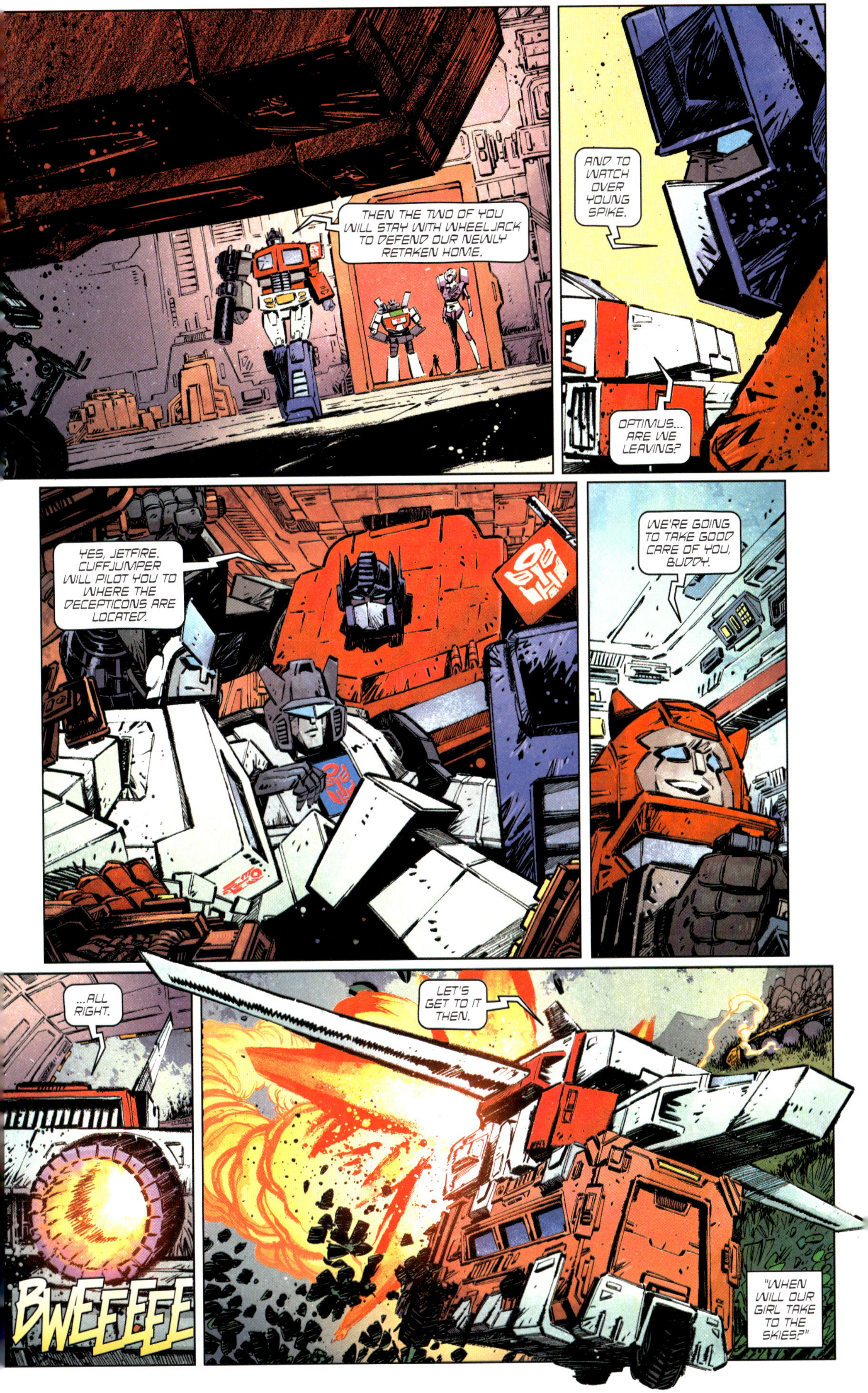
THEN THE TWO OF YOU WILL STAY WITH WHEELJACK TO DEFEND OUR NEWLY RETAKEN HOME.
AND TO WATCH OVER YOUNG SPIKE.
OPTIMUS... ARE WE LEAVING?
YES, JETFIRE. CUFFJUMPER WILL PILOT YOU TO WHERE THE DECEPTICONS ARE LOCATED.
WE'RE GOING TO TAKE GOOD CARE OF YOU, BUDDY.
...ALL RIGHT.
BWEEEEE
LET'S GET TO IT THEN.
"WHEN WILL OUR GIRL TAKE TO THE SKIES?"

THIS SHIP WILL NEVER FLY AGAIN. SHE IS TOO BIG AND NEEDS TOO MUCH ENERGON.
BUT WE ONLY NEED HER ANTENNAE.
IT'S TIME TO CALL IN REINFORCEMENTS.
SOUNDWAVE?
IS THAT REALLY YOU?

HE PACIFIC OCEAN.
MASSIVE ENERGON READINGS BELOW US, OPTIMUS!
BRING US IN CLOSER, CLIFFJUMPER!
HANG ON!
"SHOCKWAVE..."
I THANK YOU FOR YOUR WILLINGNESS TO HELP US.
YOUR THANKS IS WELCOMED, SOUNDWAVE, BUT UNNECESSARY. MY LONG-LOST BROTHERS ARE NOW FOUND! AND LOOK AT THE ABUNDANCE OF RICHES YOU HAVE STUMBLED UPON! WE WILL SOON BE CELEBRATING IN THE HALLS OF MY STRONGHOLD.
CYBERTRON'S NEW DAWN IS SOON UPON US!
BREEEE
CHAK
AGREED, DEAR BROTHER.
BRAWMMMZZKKKK
LET US BEGIN.

MAN, EARTH IS WEIRD--
WE'RE ALMOST THERE--
WAIT, CUFF, PULL UP--!
BZOOOWMMMMM
LOOK OUT--!
AGHH!
VHOMMMMMMMMM
WHAT HIT US?!
SOME SORT OF ENERGY PULSE--
WE'VE LOST THE BEAT!!

WE'RE GOING DOWN!
KRRKKRROMMM
AUTOBOTS...
TAKE COVER!
CONSTRUCTICONS! OPEN FIRE!!!
AGH...
MY, MY, MY.

THE RABBLE ROUSERS ARE STILL FIGHTING BACK, I SEE.
VHOOOH WOHMMMM
OH, NO...
WE DECEPTICONS HAVE WORK TO DO.

BZOW BZOW BZOW
YOU AUTOBOT SCUM ARE INTERRUPTING OUR GLORIOUS MISSION!
CHOOM!
CHOOM
WE HAVE SUCCEEDED, BROTHER.
INDEED.
CHEE
CHO
CHK
KIAK
CHEE
LET US BE DONE WITH THIS FOOLISHNESS.
CLIFF!
SKROWWW!

R-RATCHET?
-HKKK-
-KKK- CLIFF--
HELP--
RATCHET, **NO!**
HAHAHA! THIS TICKLES ME PURPLE, SOUNDWAVE! ONE LESS RED DEMON TO--

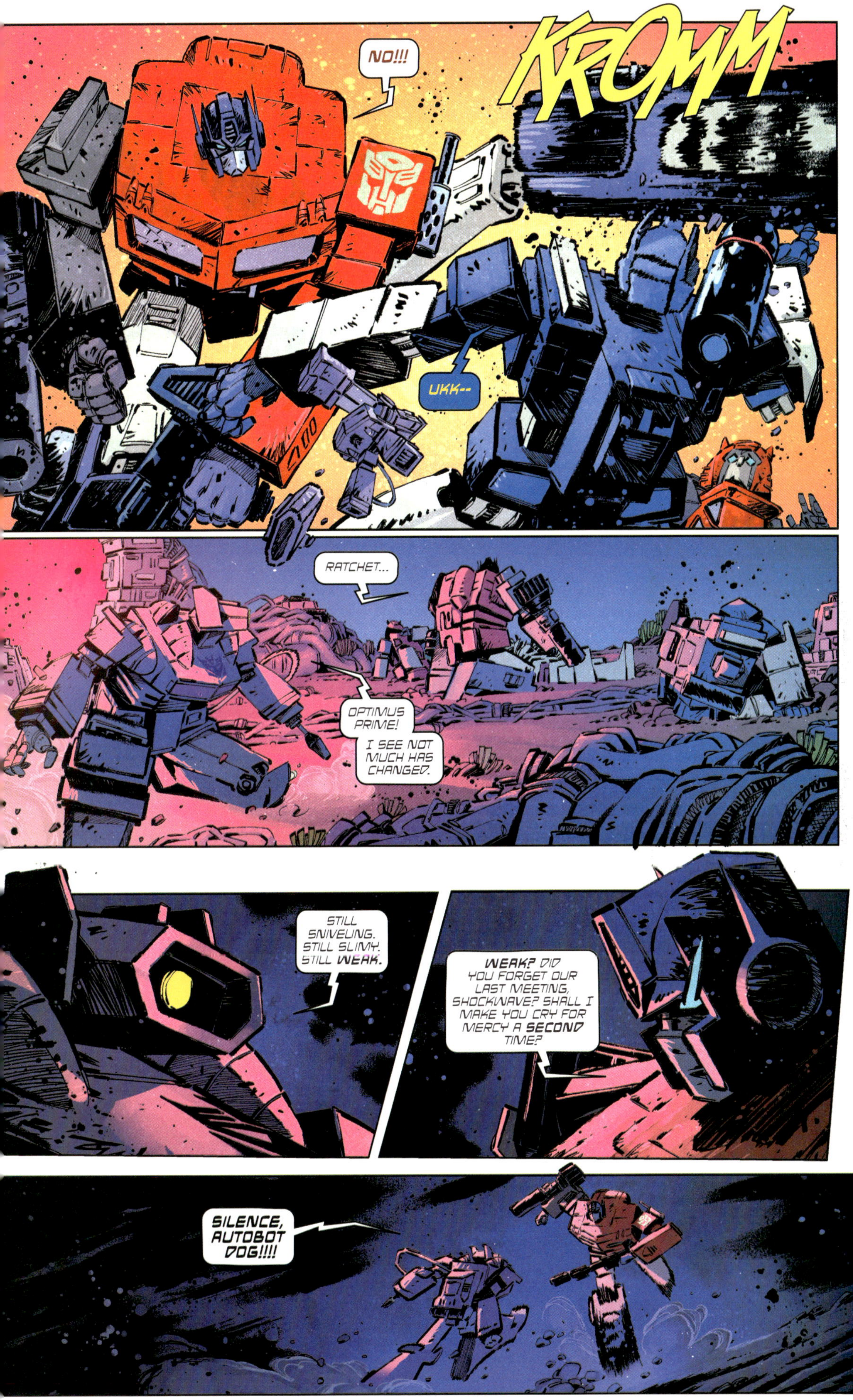
NO!!!
KROMM
UKK--
RATCHET...
OPTIMUS PRIME!
I SEE NOT MUCH HAS CHANGED.
STILL SNIVELING. STILL SLIMY. STILL WEAK.
WEAK? DID YOU FORGET OUR LAST MEETING, SHOCKWAVE? SHALL I MAKE YOU CRY FOR MERCY A SECOND TIME?
SILENCE, AUTOBOT DOG!!!!

BUT--WHEN DO WE LEARN HOW TO FIGHT?
IN TIME, CARLY. BEING LINKED IS LESS ABOUT COMBAT, AND MORE ABOUT...LOOKING OUT FOR EACH OTHER. LIKE TWO TOWERS, SEEING THEIR WORLD FROM DIFFERENT ANGLES.
THAT MAKES NO SENSE.
WE'RE ONE MILE OUT FROM THE DAM!
THINK YOU CAN GET OUR MACHINE BACK UP AND RUNNING, WHEELJACK?
I'VE GOT SOME EXTRA SUPPLIES FROM THE ARK. WITH A LITTLE LUCK, WE SHOULD HAVE ENOUGH ENERGON TO BRING MORE OF OUR FRIENDS BACK--
RATTATATA
RATTATATA
YEOW!!!
GET BACK!!!
WHO ARE YOU GUYS?
YOU'RE NOT GONNA GET THE DROP ON US TWICE, METAL MA--LADY!
STOP! PUT YOUR GUNS DOWN!
CARLY?! IS THAT YOU? WHAT ARE YOU DOING WITH THESE MONSTROSITIES?
I CAN EXPLAIN EVERYTHING! THESE ARE THE GOOD GUYS!
GOOD GUYS, HUH?
WE MEAN YOU NO HARM.
THAT'S AN AUTOBOT PROMISE.

EMERGENCY
HEY, DOC. GOOD NEWS?
NOT GREAT, I'M AFRAID.
OH.
YOUR SPINE WAS GRAZED WHEN YOU WERE SHOT, SPIKE. THIS IS SOMETHING WE CAN WORK ON, BUT...
JUST TELL ME.
AM I GONNA WALK AGAIN?
ONE THING I'VE LEARNED WHILE DOING THIS WORK, IS TO NEVER SAY NEVER. WE JUST FOUND OUT THERE ARE GIANT ROBOTS IN SPACE! ANYTHING CAN HAPPEN. DON'T GET DIS--
BOOM
WHAT'S GOING ON?
ANOTHER ONE, DOC! IT NEVER ENDS!
WHERE IS THE ONE WITH THE TALL HAIR?

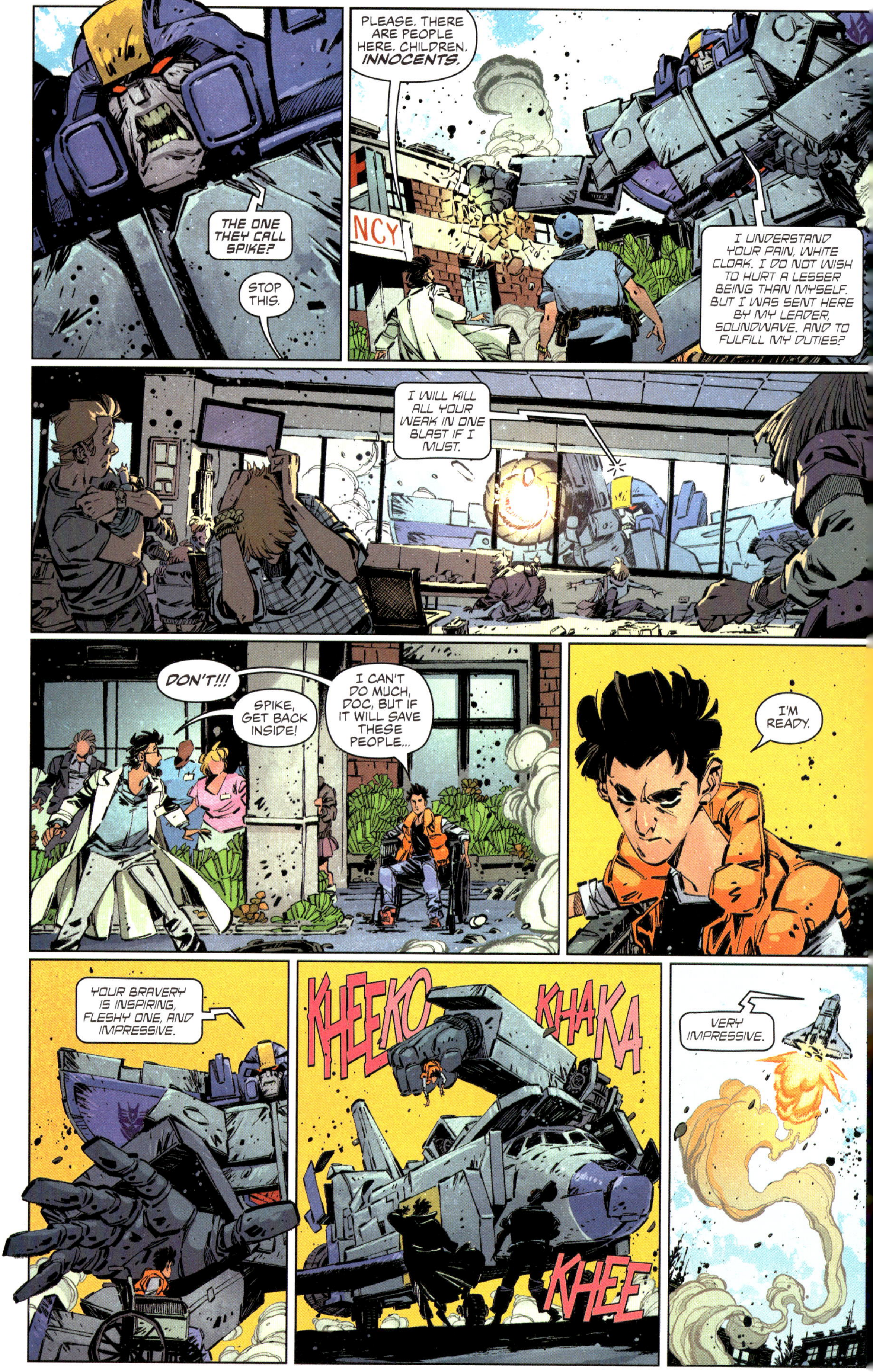
THE ONE THEY CALL SPIKE?
STOP THIS.
PLEASE. THERE ARE PEOPLE HERE. CHILDREN. INNOCENTS.
NCY
I UNDERSTAND YOUR PAIN, WHITE CLOAK. I DO NOT WISH TO HURT A LESSER BEING THAN MYSELF. BUT I WAS SENT HERE BY MY LEADER, SOUNDWAVE. AND TO FULFILL MY DUTIES?
I WILL KILL ALL YOUR WEAK IN ONE BLAST IF I MUST.
DON'T!!!
SPIKE, GET BACK INSIDE!
I CAN'T DO MUCH, DOC, BUT IF IT WILL SAVE THESE PEOPLE...
I'M READY.
YOUR BRAVERY IS INSPIRING, FLESHY ONE, AND IMPRESSIVE.
KHEEKO
KHAKA
KHEE
VERY IMPRESSIVE.

BOOM
HANG ON, OPTIM--
GYAGGHH!
THANK YOU FOR THE ASSIST, SCRAPPER!
FOR THE CAUSE, MY GENERAL!
CHOMMM
YOU FOUGHT DIRTY LAST TIME, OPTIMUS. BUT I HAVE LEARNED MUCH SINCE THAT DAY.

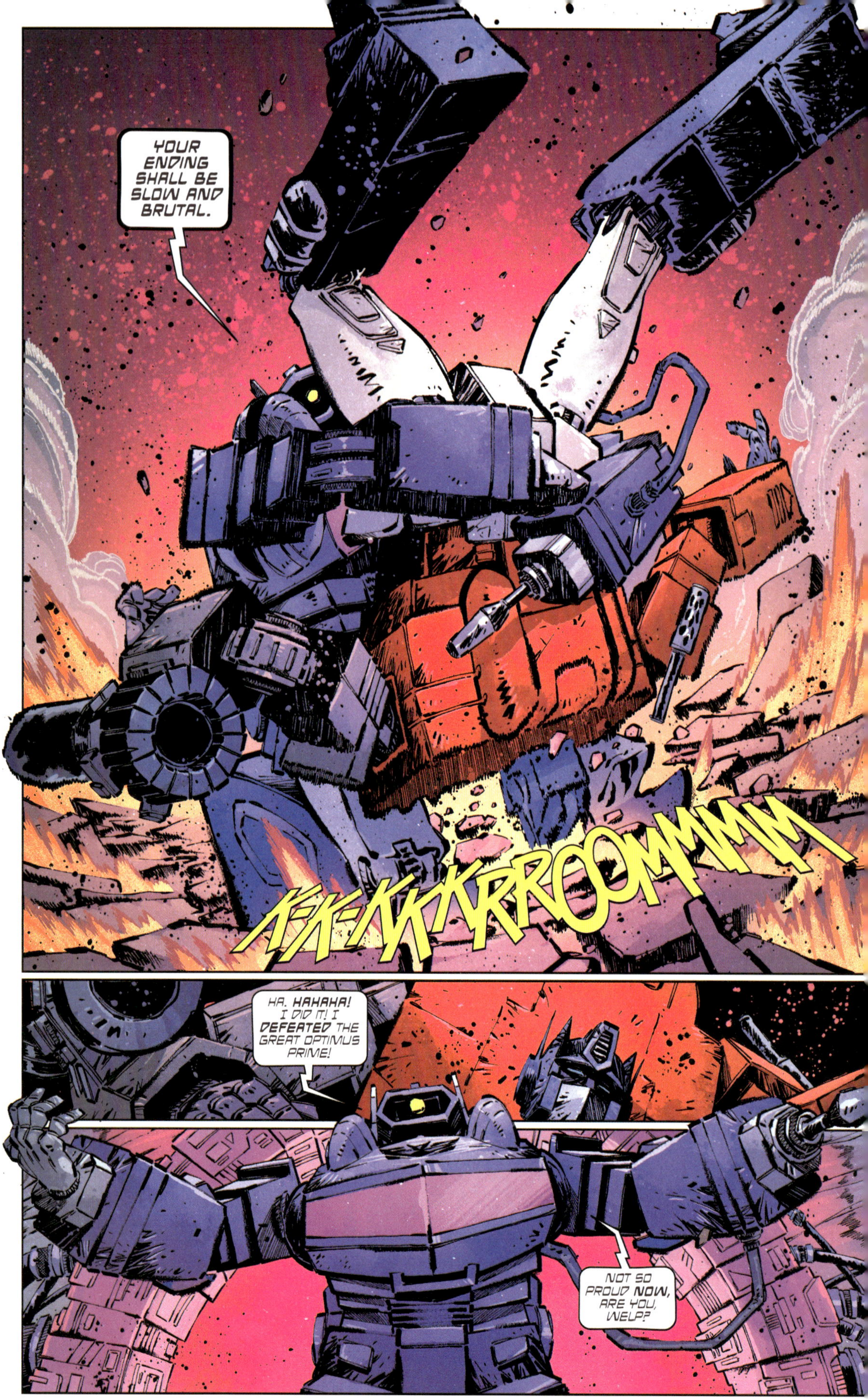
YOUR ENDING SHALL BE SLOW AND BRUTAL.
K-K-KKKRROOMMMM
HA. **HAHAHA!** I DID IT! I **DEFEATED** THE GREAT OPTIMUS PRIME!
NOT SO PROUD **NOW**, ARE YOU, WELP?

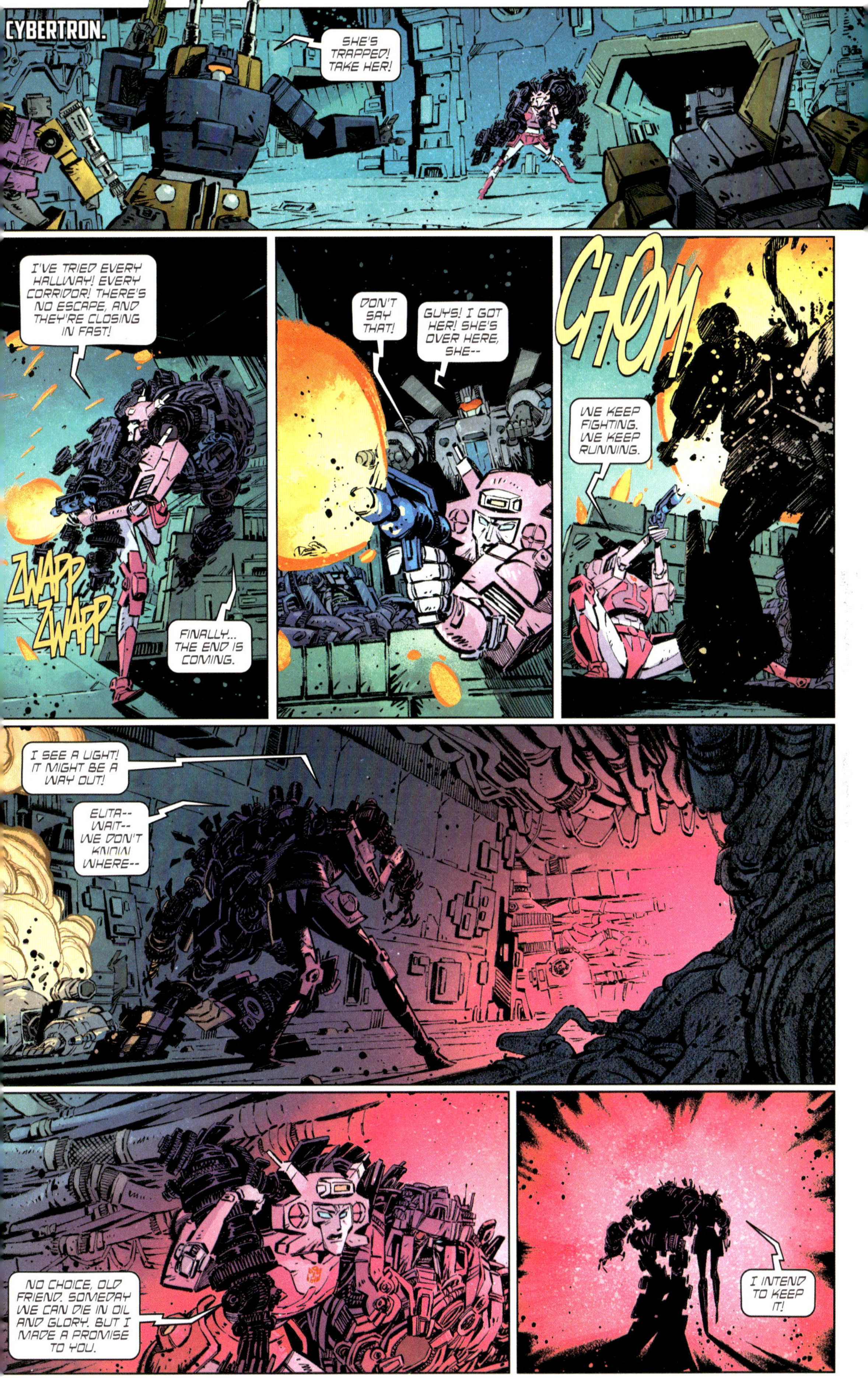

CYBERTRON.
SHE'S TRAPPED! TAKE HER!
I'VE TRIED EVERY HALLWAY! EVERY CORRIDOR! THERE'S NO ESCAPE, AND THEY'RE CLOSING IN FAST!
ZWAPP ZWAPP
FINALLY... THE END IS COMING.
DON'T SAY THAT!
GUYS! I GOT HER! SHE'S OVER HERE, SHE--
CHOM
WE KEEP FIGHTING. WE KEEP RUNNING.
I SEE A LIGHT! IT MIGHT BE A WAY OUT!
ELITA-- WAIT-- WE DON'T KNOW WHERE--
NO CHOICE, OLD FRIEND. SOMEDAY WE CAN DIE IN OIL AND GLORY. BUT I MADE A PROMISE TO YOU.
I INTEND TO KEEP IT!

KRROOOOMMM
...OPTIMUS?!
WHAT IS THIS PLACE--
COMBATICONS!
MERGE TO FORM--

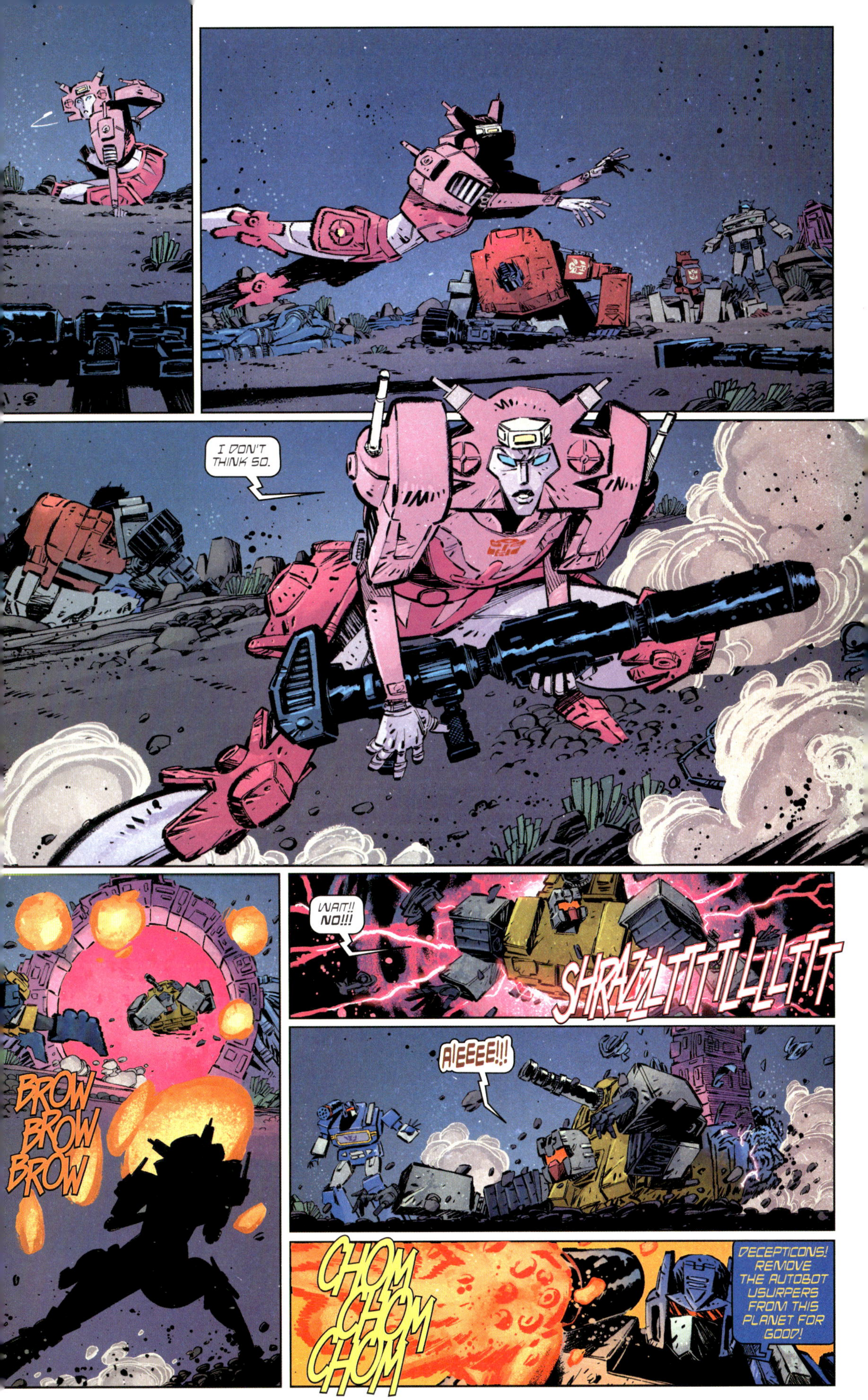
I DON'T THINK SO.
BROW BROW BROW
WAIT!! NO!!!
SHRAZZLTTTTLLLLTTT
AIEEEE!!!
CHOM CHOM CHOM
DECEPTICONS! REMOVE THE AUTOBOT USURPERS FROM THIS PLANET FOR GOOD!

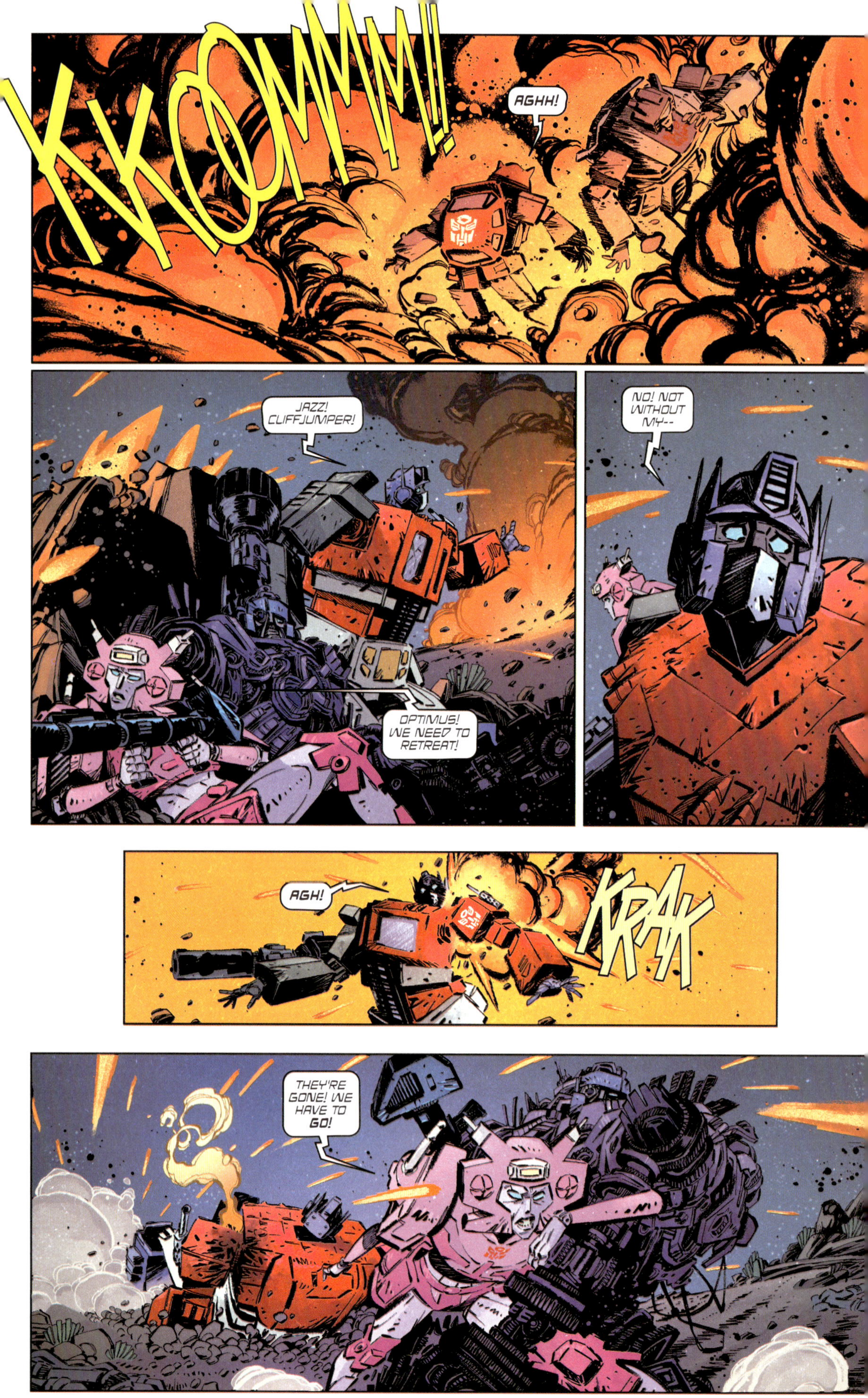
KKOOMMM!!!
AGHH!
JAZZ! CLIFFJUMPER!
OPTIMUS! WE NEED TO RETREAT!
NO! NOT WITHOUT MY--
AGH!
KRAK
THEY'RE GONE! WE HAVE TO GO!

TRANSFORM--
CHEE CHAKHO KA
FWUMP
CHOOM
AND ROLL OUT!
DECEPTICONS, PREPARE TO GIVE CH--
NO, SOUNDWAVE.
LET THEM GO. WE MUST FOCUS ON REPAIRING THE LINK BETWEEN OUR TWO WORLDS. THE AUTOBOTS ARE NOW MERE ANTS IN RELATION TO OUR PLAN.
OP... OPTIMUS...?
OH, HO! LOOK AT THESE GIFTS FROM PRIMUS!

THESE AUTOBOTS HAVE BEEN ON THIS PLANET FOR MANY YEARS. I MUST CONDUCT EXPERIMENTS ON THE EFFECT THIS HAS HAD ON THEM.
UH... EXPERIMENTS?
OH, YES.
...WAIT...
PAINFUL EXPERIMENTS.
NOOOO!

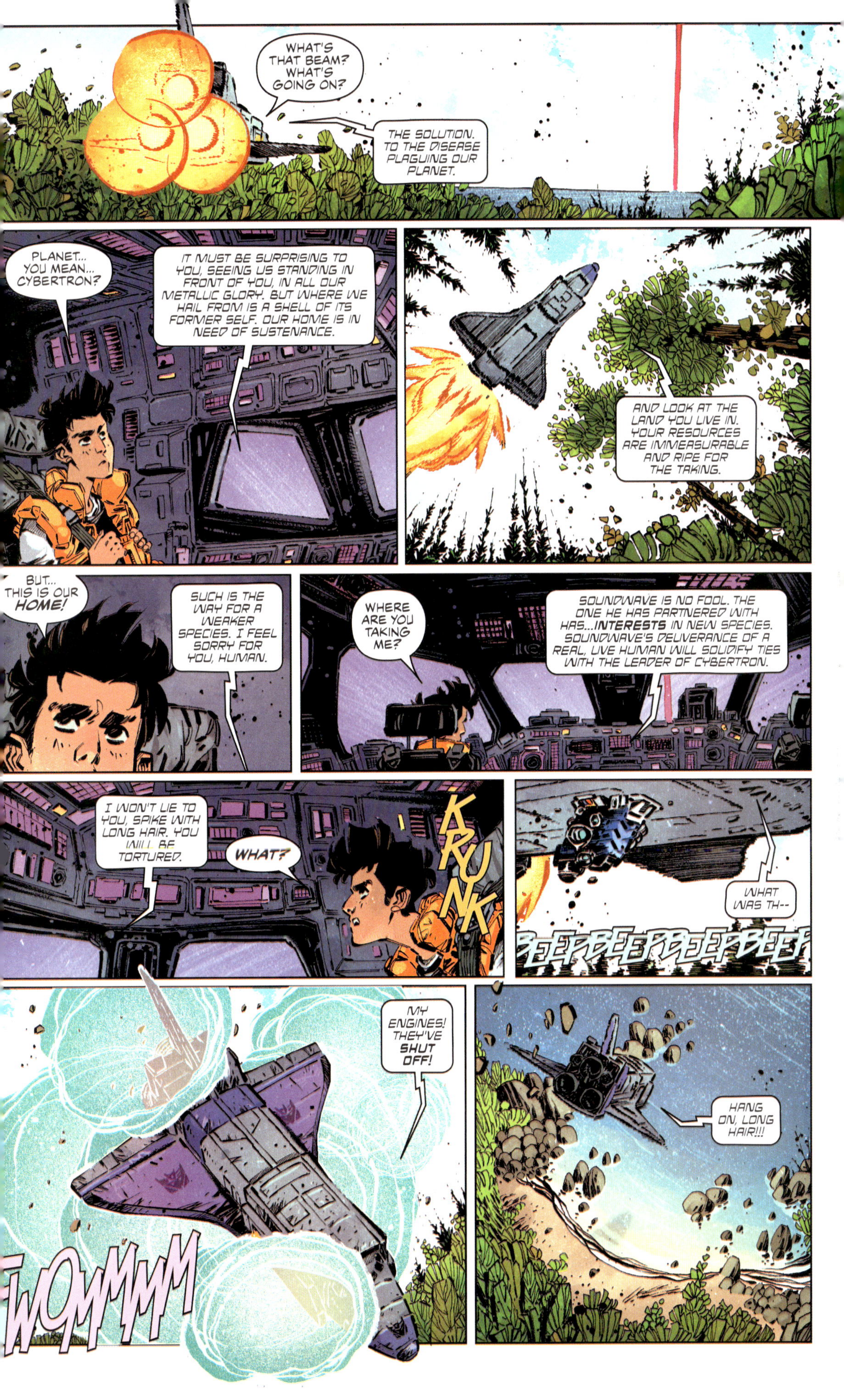
WHAT'S THAT BEAM? WHAT'S GOING ON?
THE SOLUTION. TO THE DISEASE PLAGUING OUR PLANET.
PLANET... YOU MEAN... CYBERTRON?
IT MUST BE SURPRISING TO YOU, SEEING US STANDING IN FRONT OF YOU, IN ALL OUR METALLIC GLORY. BUT WHERE WE HAIL FROM IS A SHELL OF ITS FORMER SELF. OUR HOME IS IN NEED OF SUSTENANCE.
AND LOOK AT THE LAND YOU LIVE IN. YOUR RESOURCES ARE IMMEASURABLE AND RIPE FOR THE TAKING.
BUT... THIS IS OUR HOME!
SUCH IS THE WAY FOR A WEAKER SPECIES. I FEEL SORRY FOR YOU, HUMAN.
WHERE ARE YOU TAKING ME?
SOUNDWAVE IS NO FOOL. THE ONE HE HAS PARTNERED WITH HAS...INTERESTS IN NEW SPECIES. SOUNDWAVE'S DELIVERANCE OF A REAL, LIVE HUMAN WILL SOLIDIFY TIES WITH THE LEADER OF CYBERTRON.
I WON'T LIE TO YOU, SPIKE WITH LONG HAIR. YOU WILL BE TORTURED.
WHAT?
KRUNK
WHAT WAS TH--
BEEPBEEPBEEPBEEPBEEP
MY ENGINES! THEY'VE SHUT OFF!
WOMMMM
HANG ON, LONG HAIR!!!

WHOMMMM
KRRKKKKKK
YOUR NAME IS SPIKE, YES?
WHO?!
MY NAME IS BEACHCOMBER. I'M HERE TO RESCUE YOU.

EARTH ORBIT.
MILLIONS OF YEARS AGO.
AUTOBOT TRASH!
S-STOP!
N--
ENJOY YOUR TIME TRAVELING THE STARS!
WHOOOSH

UNITED STATES

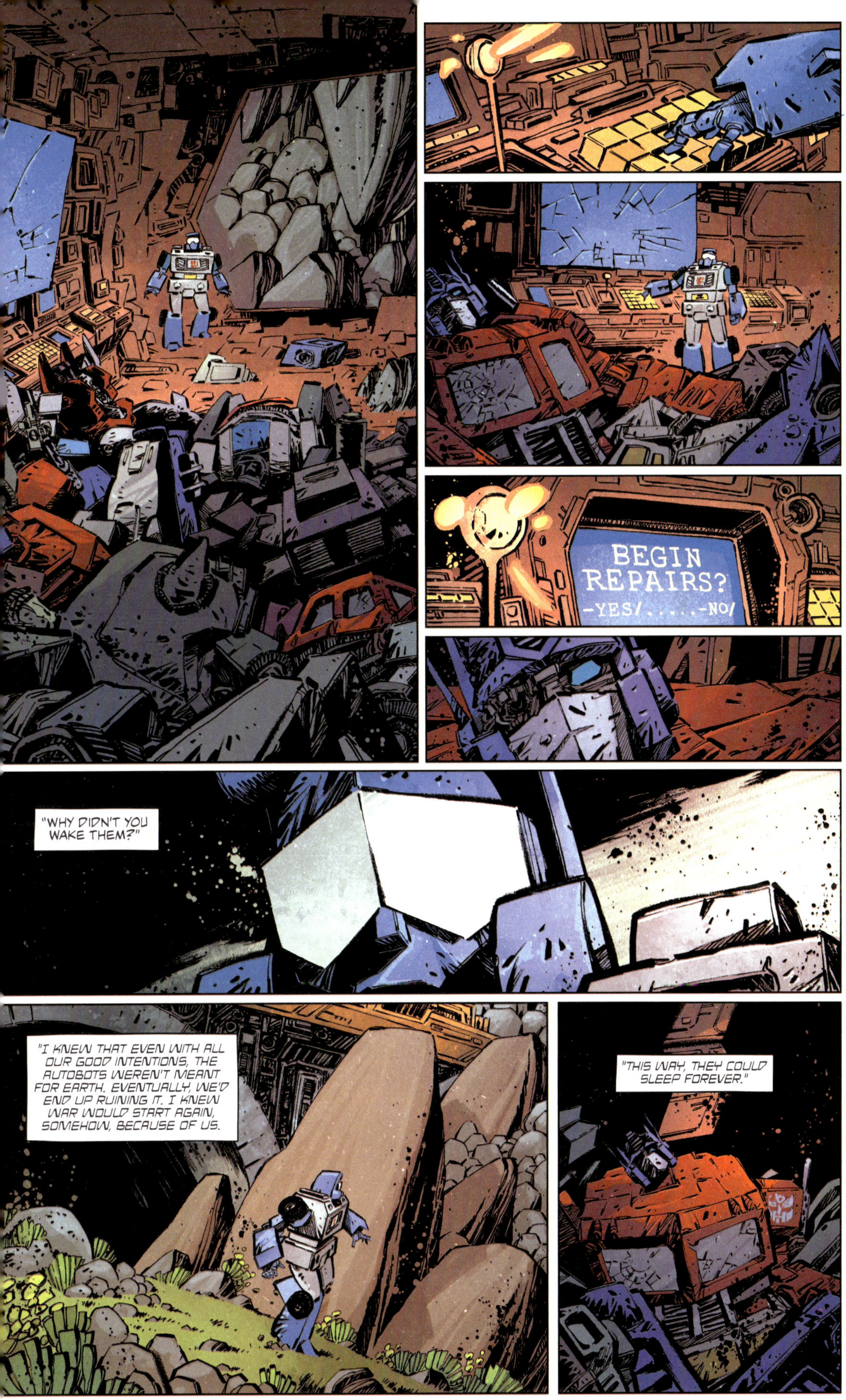
BEGIN REPAIRS?
-YES/.....-NO/
"WHY DIDN'T YOU WAKE THEM?"
"I KNEW THAT EVEN WITH ALL OUR GOOD INTENTIONS, THE AUTOBOTS WEREN'T MEANT FOR EARTH. EVENTUALLY, WE'D END UP RUINING IT. I KNEW WAR WOULD START AGAIN, SOMEHOW, BECAUSE OF US.
"THIS WAY, THEY COULD SLEEP FOREVER."

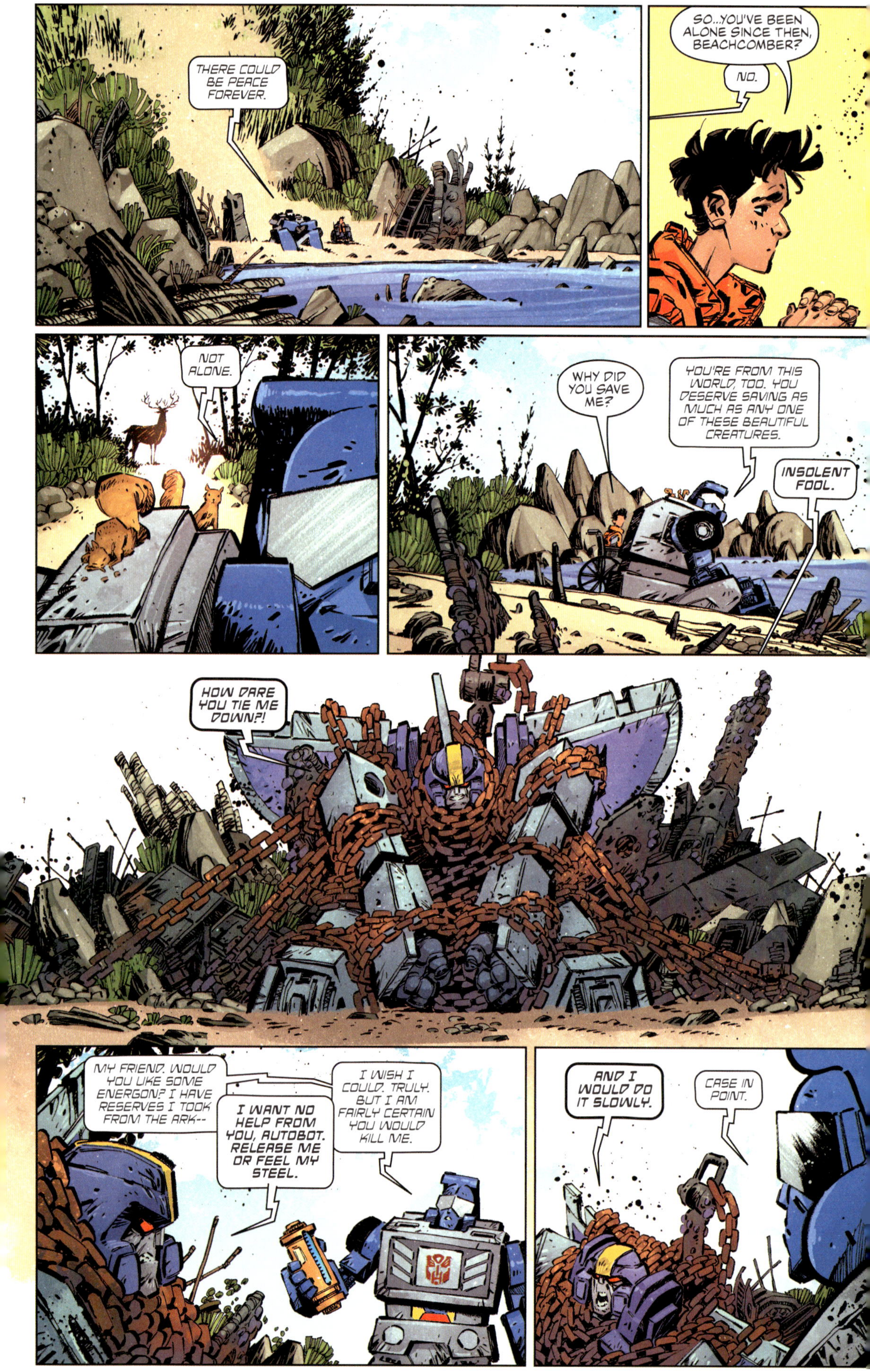
THERE COULD BE PEACE FOREVER.
SO...YOU'VE BEEN ALONE SINCE THEN, BEACHCOMBER?
NO.
NOT ALONE.
WHY DID YOU SAVE ME?
YOU'RE FROM THIS WORLD, TOO. YOU DESERVE SAVING AS MUCH AS ANY ONE OF THESE BEAUTIFUL CREATURES.
INSOLENT FOOL.
HOW DARE YOU TIE ME DOWN?!
MY FRIEND. WOULD YOU LIKE SOME ENERGON? I HAVE RESERVES I TOOK FROM THE ARK--
I WANT NO HELP FROM YOU, AUTOBOT. RELEASE ME OR FEEL MY STEEL.
I WISH I COULD. TRULY. BUT I AM FAIRLY CERTAIN YOU WOULD KILL ME.
AND I WOULD DO IT SLOWLY.
CASE IN POINT.

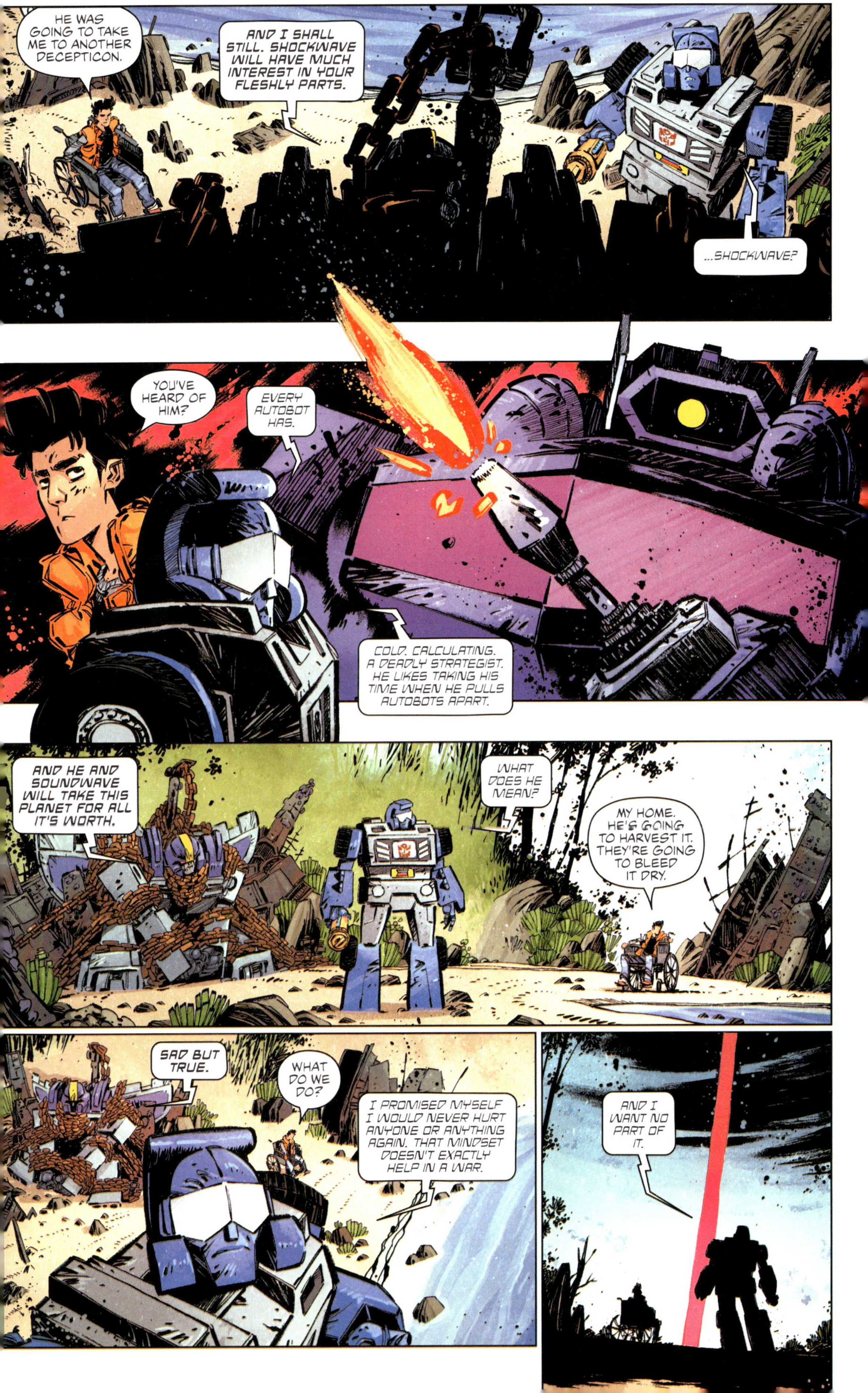
HE WAS GOING TO TAKE ME TO ANOTHER DECEPTICON.
AND I SHALL STILL. SHOCKWAVE WILL HAVE MUCH INTEREST IN YOUR FLESHLY PARTS.
...SHOCKWAVE?
YOU'VE HEARD OF HIM?
EVERY AUTOBOT HAS.
COLD. CALCULATING. A DEADLY STRATEGIST. HE LIKES TAKING HIS TIME WHEN HE PULLS AUTOBOTS APART.
AND HE AND SOUNDWAVE WILL TAKE THIS PLANET FOR ALL IT'S WORTH.
WHAT DOES HE MEAN?
MY HOME. HE'S GOING TO HARVEST IT. THEY'RE GOING TO BLEED IT DRY.
SAD BUT TRUE.
WHAT DO WE DO?
I PROMISED MYSELF I WOULD NEVER HURT ANYONE OR ANYTHING AGAIN. THAT MINDSET DOESN'T EXACTLY HELP IN A WAR.
AND I WANT NO PART OF IT.

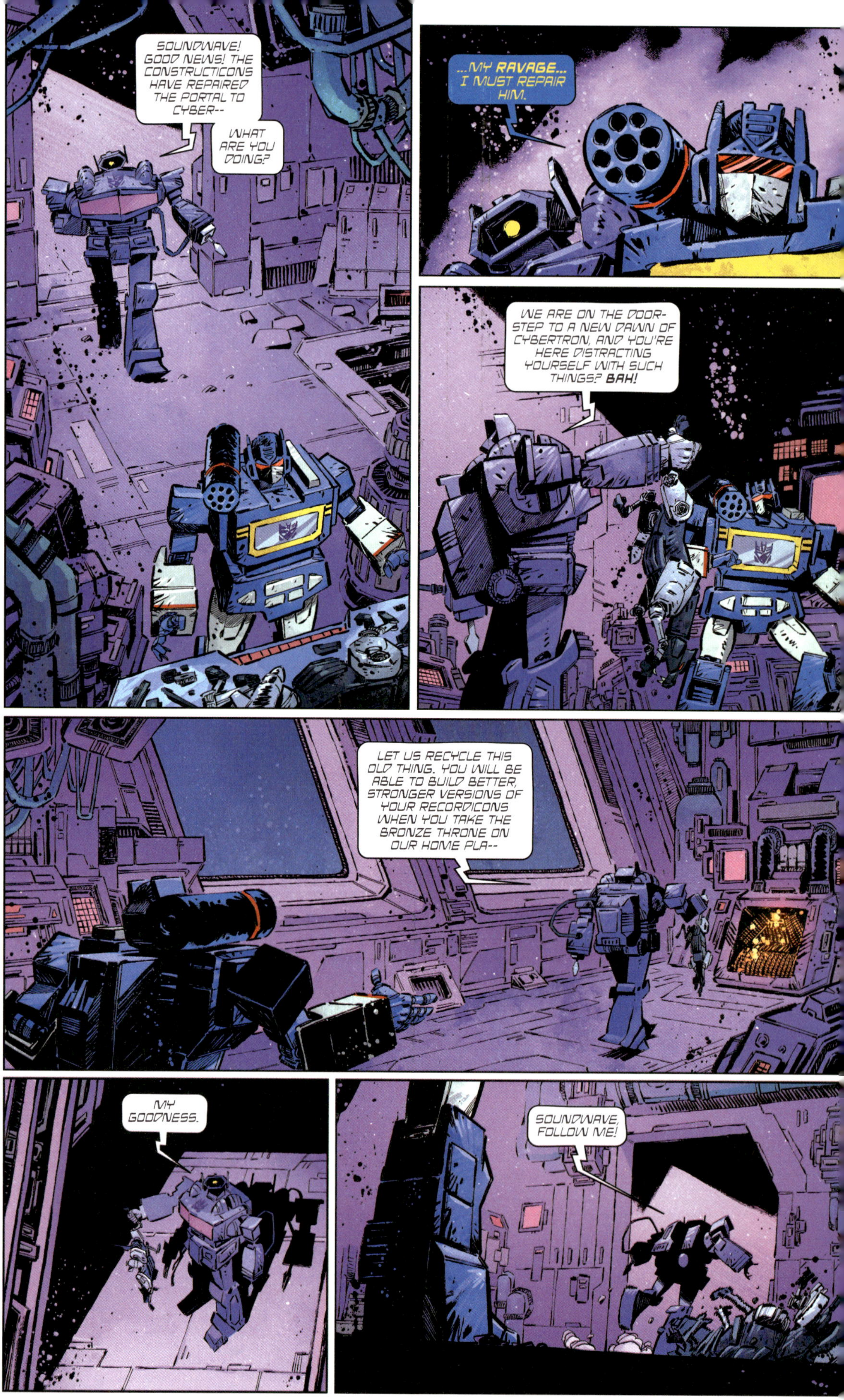
SOUNDWAVE! GOOD NEWS! THE CONSTRUCTICONS HAVE REPAIRED THE PORTAL TO CYBER--
WHAT ARE YOU DOING?
...MY RAVAGE... I MUST REPAIR HIM.
WE ARE ON THE DOORSTEP TO A NEW DAWN OF CYBERTRON, AND YOU'RE HERE DISTRACTING YOURSELF WITH SUCH THINGS? BAH!
LET US RECYCLE THIS OLD THING. YOU WILL BE ABLE TO BUILD BETTER, STRONGER VERSIONS OF YOUR RECORDICONS WHEN YOU TAKE THE BRONZE THRONE ON OUR HOME PLA--
MY GOODNESS.
SOUNDWAVE, FOLLOW ME!

UNBELIEVABLE!
HAVE YOU EVER SEEN ANYTHING SO MAJESTIC?
THIS PLANET HAS MANY ORGANIC WONDERS. THERE IS SOMETHING NEW TO SEE EVERY DAY.
ISN'T IT WONDERFUL TO KNOW THIS BEAUTY WILL AID SUCH A WONDERFUL CAUSE?
COMMANDER SHOCKWAVE!

THE **FEEDER** IS PREPPED AND READY!
VERY GOOD.
VRM VRM VRM VRM VRM
YES!
YES! YESSSS!

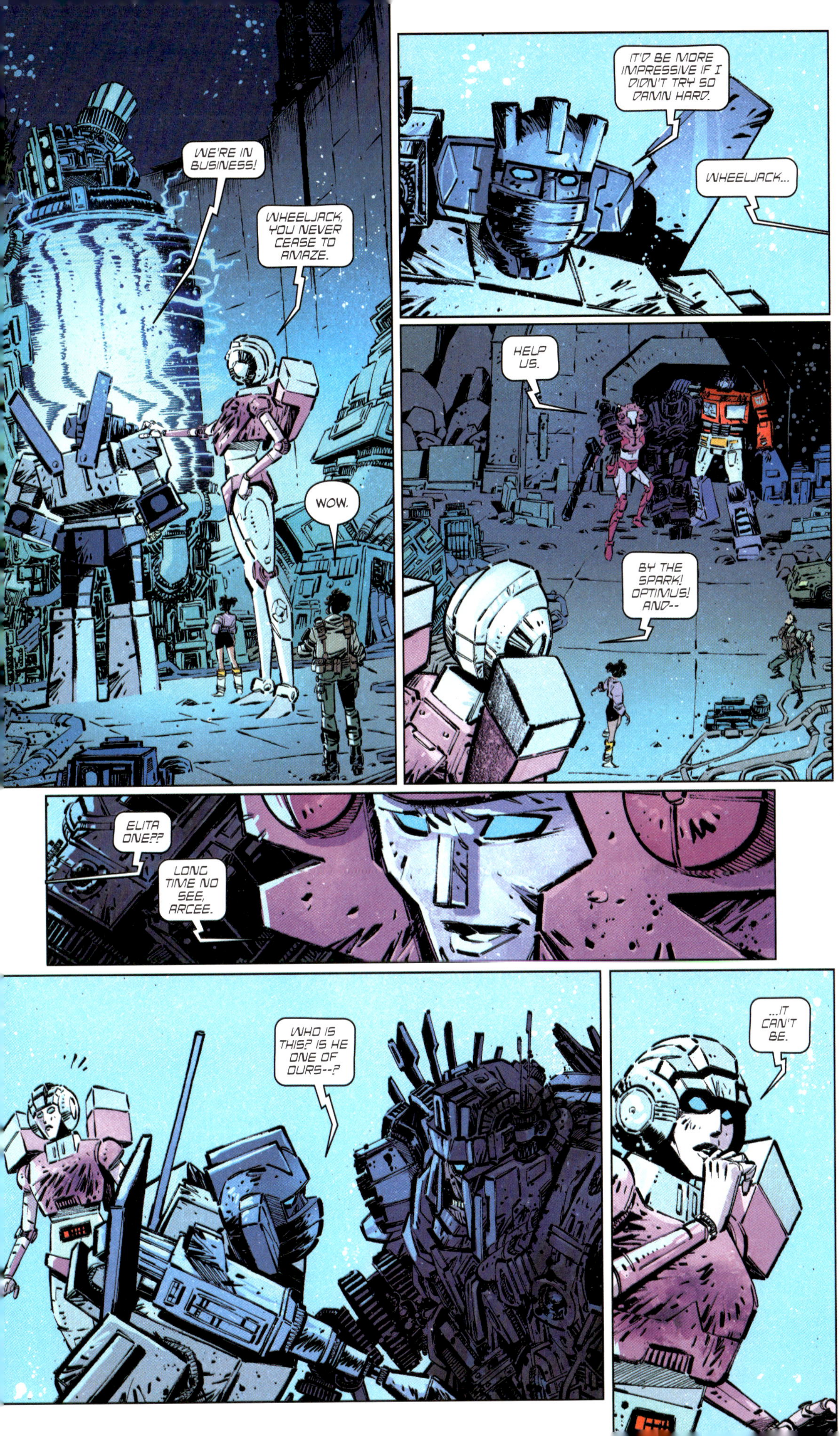
WE'RE IN BUSINESS!
WHEELJACK, YOU NEVER CEASE TO AMAZE.
WOW.
IT'D BE MORE IMPRESSIVE IF I DIDN'T TRY SO DAMN HARD.
WHEELJACK...
HELP US.
BY THE SPARK! OPTIMUS! AND--
ELITA ONE??
LONG TIME NO SEE, ARCEE.
WHO IS THIS? IS HE ONE OF OURS--?
...IT CAN'T BE.

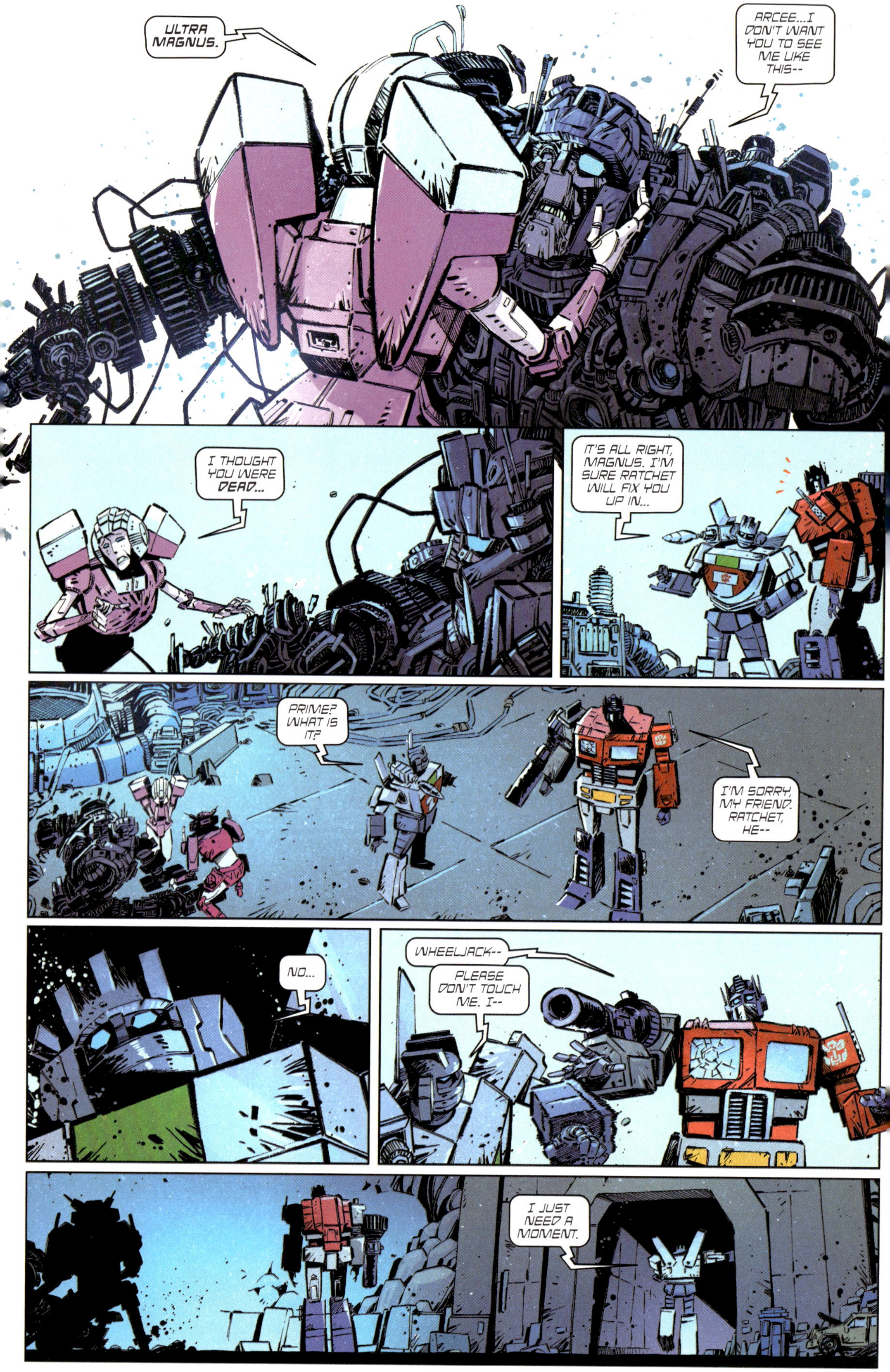
ULTRA MAGNUS.
ARCEE...I DON'T WANT YOU TO SEE ME LIKE THIS--
I THOUGHT YOU WERE DEAD...
IT'S ALL RIGHT, MAGNUS. I'M SURE RATCHET WILL FIX YOU UP IN...
PRIME? WHAT IS IT?
I'M SORRY, MY FRIEND. RATCHET, HE--
NO...
WHEELJACK--
PLEASE DON'T TOUCH ME. I--
I JUST NEED A MOMENT.

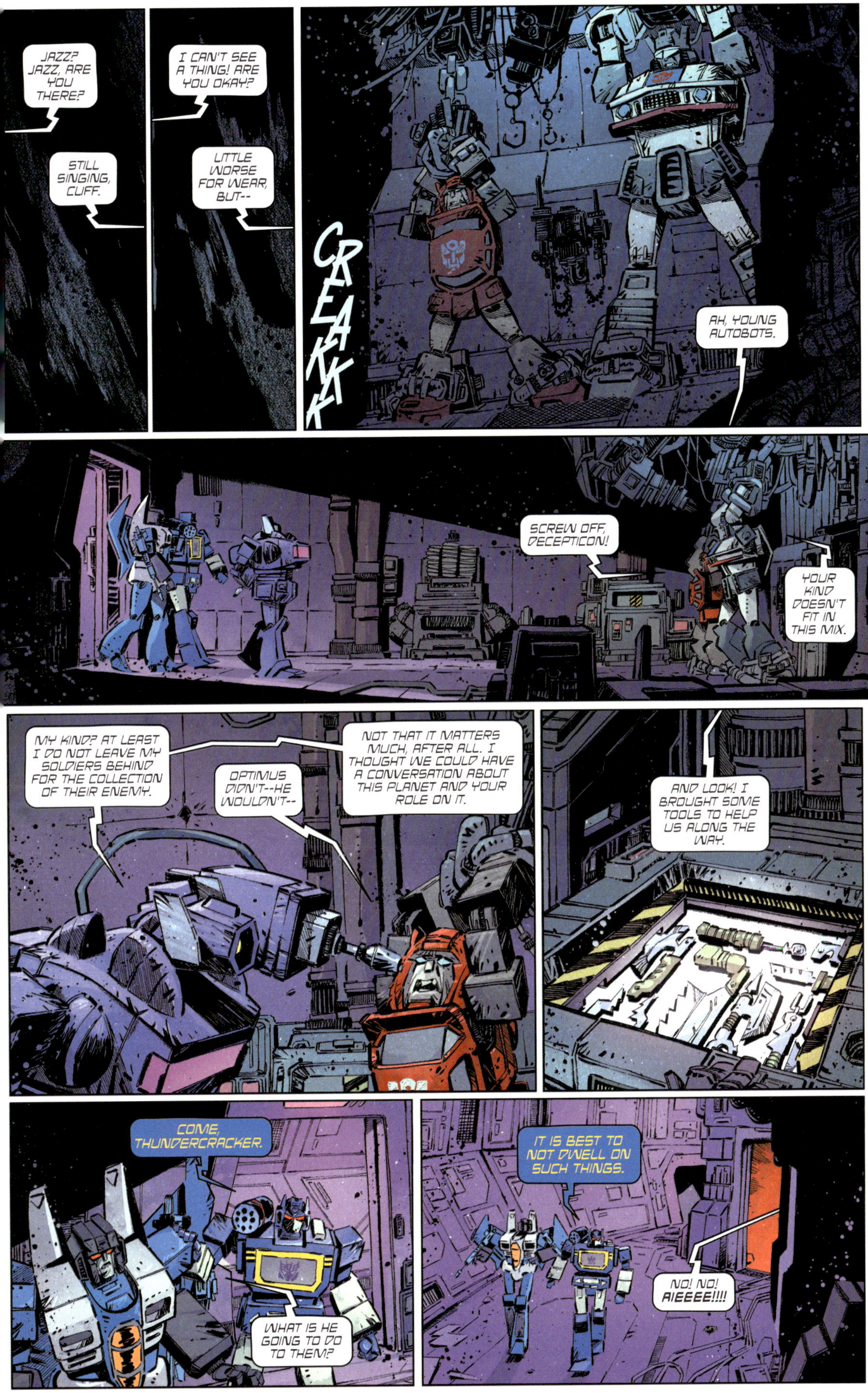
JAZZ? JAZZ, ARE YOU THERE?
STILL SINGING, CLIFF.
I CAN'T SEE A THING! ARE YOU OKAY?
LITTLE WORSE FOR WEAR, BUT--
CREAKK
AH, YOUNG AUTOBOTS.
SCREW OFF, DECEPTICON!
YOUR KIND DOESN'T FIT IN THIS MIX.
MY KIND? AT LEAST I DO NOT LEAVE MY SOLDIERS BEHIND FOR THE COLLECTION OF THEIR ENEMY.
OPTIMUS DIDN'T--HE WOULDN'T--
NOT THAT IT MATTERS MUCH, AFTER ALL. I THOUGHT WE COULD HAVE A CONVERSATION ABOUT THIS PLANET AND YOUR ROLE ON IT.
AND LOOK! I BROUGHT SOME TOOLS TO HELP US ALONG THE WAY.
COME, THUNDERCRACKER.
WHAT IS HE GOING TO DO TO THEM?
IT IS BEST TO NOT DWELL ON SUCH THINGS.
NO! NO! AIEEEE!!!!

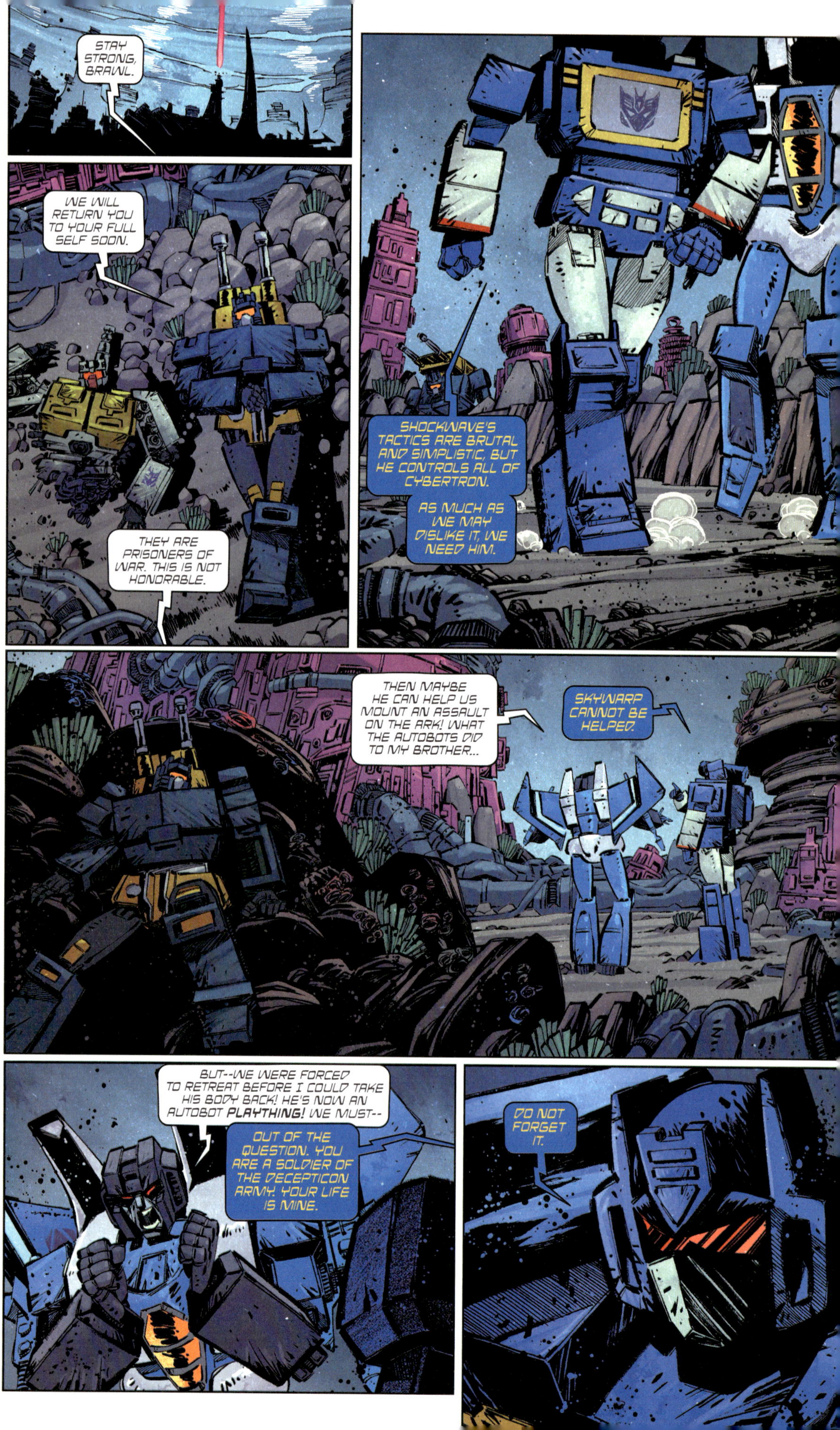
STAY STRONG, BRAWL.
WE WILL RETURN YOU TO YOUR FULL SELF SOON.
THEY ARE PRISONERS OF WAR. THIS IS NOT HONORABLE.
SHOCKWAVE'S TACTICS ARE BRUTAL AND SIMPLISTIC, BUT HE CONTROLS ALL OF CYBERTRON.
AS MUCH AS WE MAY DISLIKE IT, WE NEED HIM.
THEN MAYBE HE CAN HELP US MOUNT AN ASSAULT ON THE ARK! WHAT THE AUTOBOTS DID TO MY BROTHER...
SKYWARP CANNOT BE HELPED.
BUT--WE WERE FORCED TO RETREAT BEFORE I COULD TAKE HIS BODY BACK! HE'S NOW AN AUTOBOT PLAYTHING! WE MUST--
OUT OF THE QUESTION. YOU ARE A SOLDIER OF THE DECEPTICON ARMY. YOUR LIFE IS MINE.
DO NOT FORGET IT.

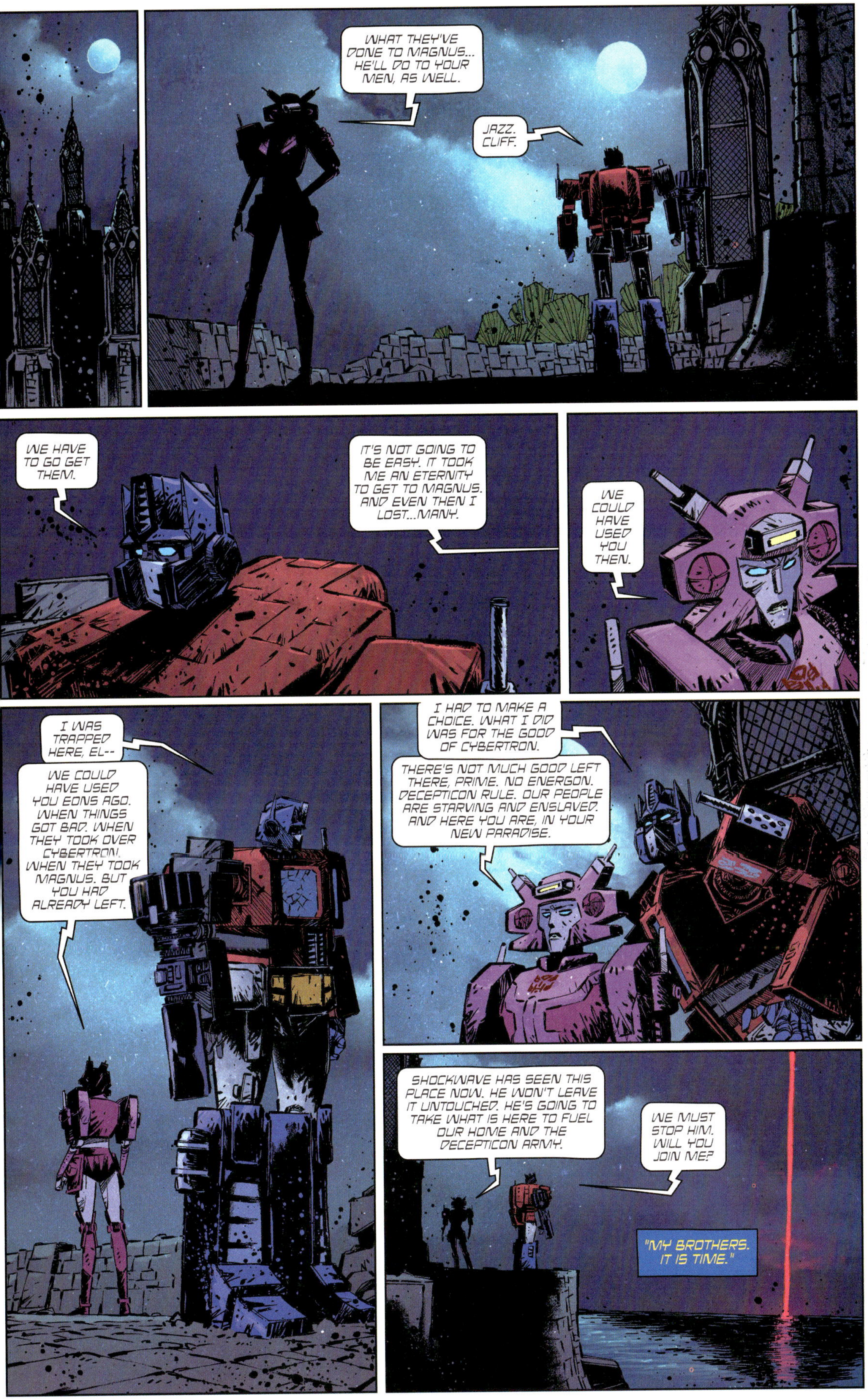
WHAT THEY'VE DONE TO MAGNUS... HE'LL DO TO YOUR MEN, AS WELL.
JAZZ. CLIFF.
WE HAVE TO GO GET THEM.
IT'S NOT GOING TO BE EASY. IT TOOK ME AN ETERNITY TO GET TO MAGNUS. AND EVEN THEN I LOST...MANY.
WE COULD HAVE USED YOU THEN.
I WAS TRAPPED HERE, EL--
WE COULD HAVE USED YOU EONS AGO. WHEN THINGS GOT BAD. WHEN THEY TOOK OVER CYBERTRON. WHEN THEY TOOK MAGNUS. BUT YOU HAD ALREADY LEFT.
I HAD TO MAKE A CHOICE. WHAT I DID WAS FOR THE GOOD OF CYBERTRON.
THERE'S NOT MUCH GOOD LEFT THERE, PRIME. NO ENERGON. DECEPTICON RULE. OUR PEOPLE ARE STARVING AND ENSLAVED. AND HERE YOU ARE, IN YOUR NEW PARADISE.
SHOCKWAVE HAS SEEN THIS PLACE NOW. HE WON'T LEAVE IT UNTOUCHED. HE'S GOING TO TAKE WHAT IS HERE TO FUEL OUR HOME AND THE DECEPTICON ARMY.
WE MUST STOP HIM. WILL YOU JOIN ME?
"MY BROTHERS. IT IS TIME."

HAVEN'T WE...ALREADY STARTED?
HA! GATHERING ALL THIS PLANET HAS TO OFFER WITH SUCH SMALL TECH AS THIS WOULD TAKE A CENTURY!
NO. OUR WORLD IS ON THE EDGE OF DEVASTATION. WE MUST MOVE FASTER.
BP BP BP
FWOOOSHHH
BREEEE
SKAKKKKKKK
VREEEEEEE

WAAAAAA
MUCH FASTER.
BRAKKAAAZZZZZZZ
OUR PLANET WRITHES WITH THIRST.
SHWOOOMMMMZZZZ

BWAAAAAAA

"WHY NOT BRING OUR HOME TO THE SOURCE?"

YES! THE HOUR OF OUR VICTORY HAS COME!!!
BEACHCOMBER?
CYBERTRON.
LET THE HARVEST BEGIN.

SPLSHH
CHNK
SHHHH
BRRRRR
BWAASHHHH
WHOMMM
"DO YOU REMEMBER THE FIRST TIME WE MET?"

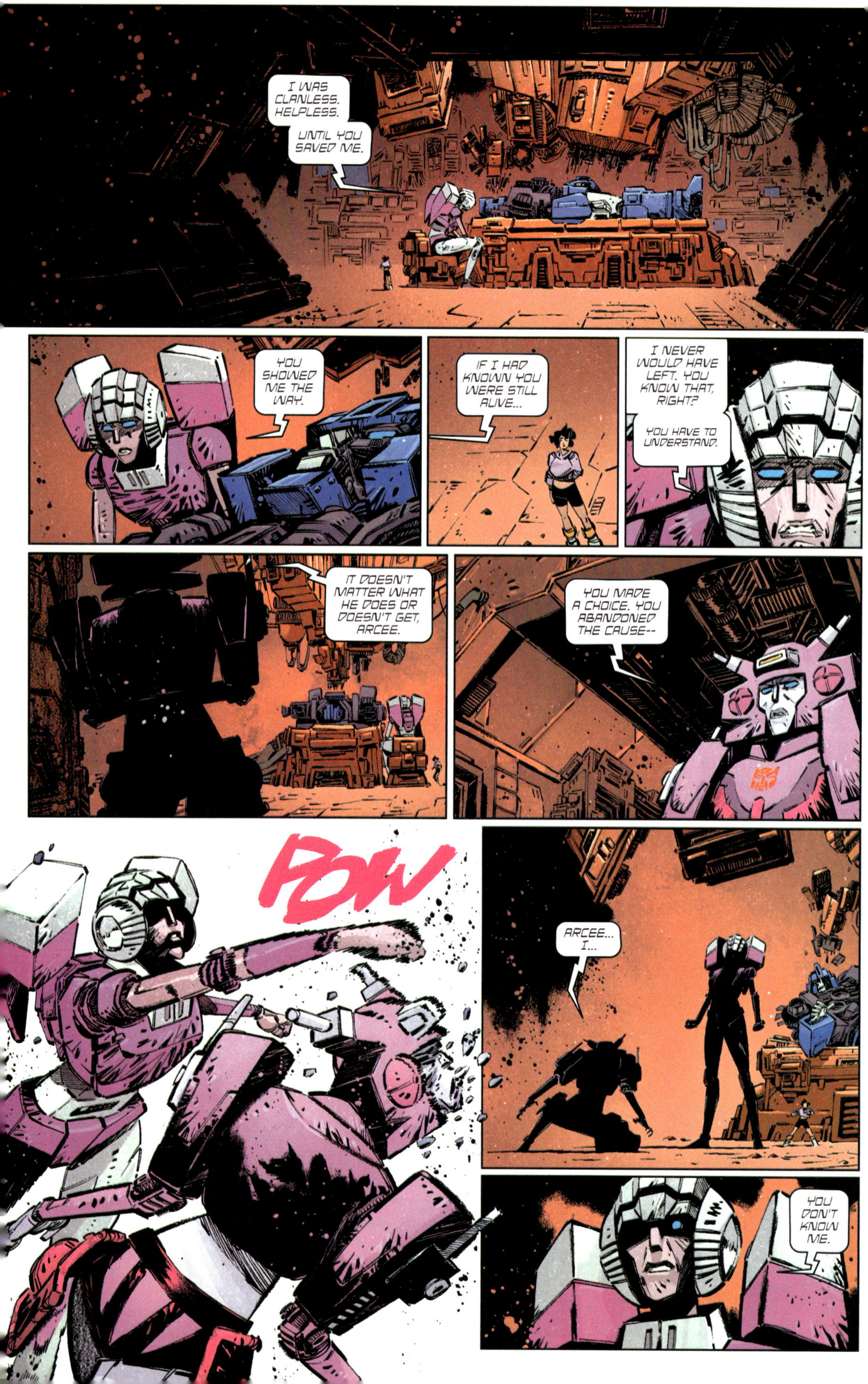
I WAS CLANLESS. HELPLESS.
UNTIL YOU SAVED ME.
YOU SHOWED ME THE WAY.
IF I HAD KNOWN YOU WERE STILL ALIVE...
I NEVER WOULD HAVE LEFT. YOU KNOW THAT, RIGHT?
YOU HAVE TO UNDERSTAND.
IT DOESN'T MATTER WHAT HE DOES OR DOESN'T GET, ARCEE.
YOU MADE A CHOICE. YOU ABANDONED THE CAUSE--
POW
ARCEE... I...
YOU DON'T KNOW ME.

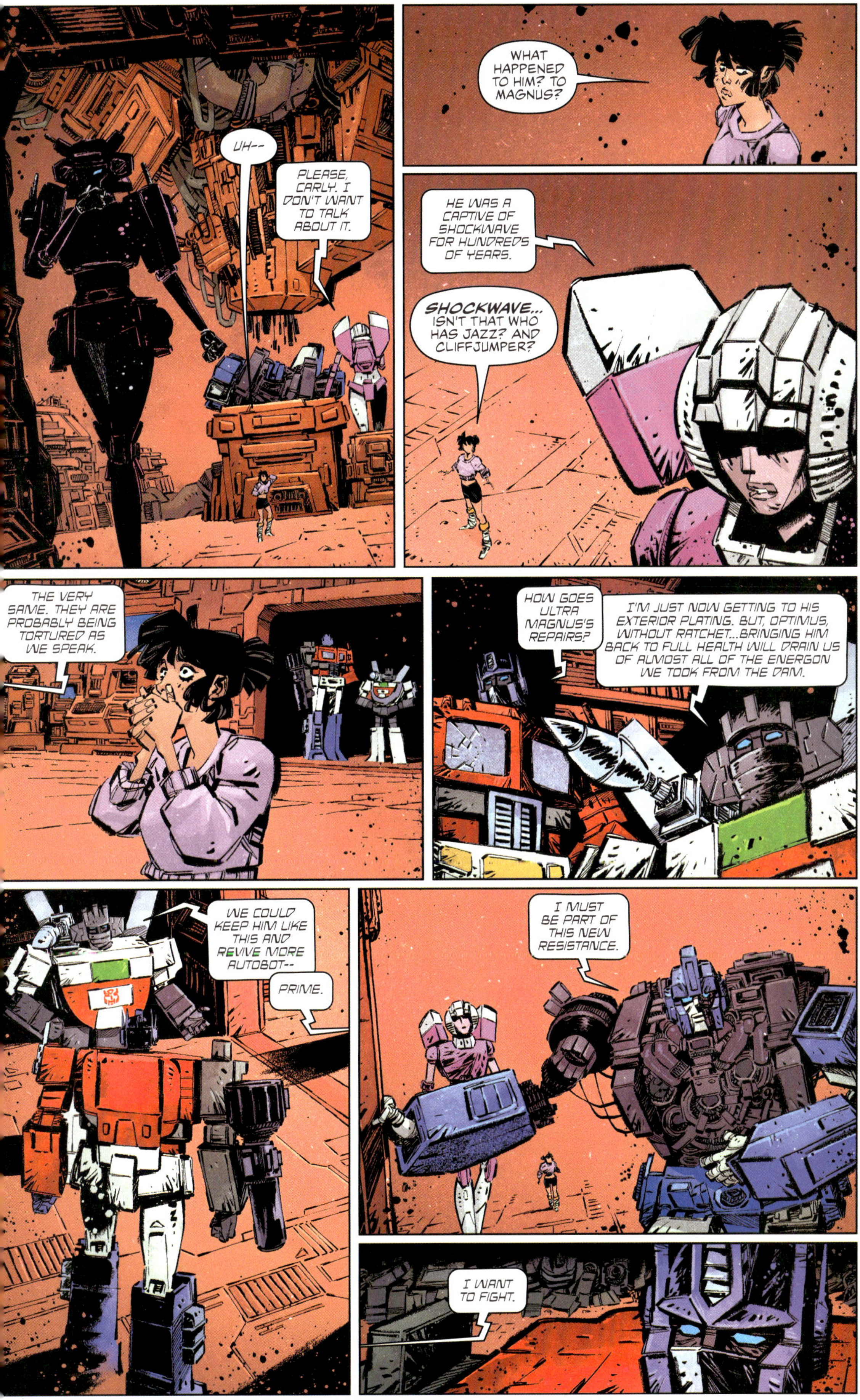
UH--
PLEASE, CARLY. I DON'T WANT TO TALK ABOUT IT.
WHAT HAPPENED TO HIM? TO MAGNUS?
HE WAS A CAPTIVE OF SHOCKWAVE FOR HUNDREDS OF YEARS.
SHOCKWAVE... ISN'T THAT WHO HAS JAZZ? AND CLIFFJUMPER?
THE VERY SAME. THEY ARE PROBABLY BEING TORTURED AS WE SPEAK.
HOW GOES ULTRA MAGNUS'S REPAIRS?
I'M JUST NOW GETTING TO HIS EXTERIOR PLATING. BUT, OPTIMUS, WITHOUT RATCHET...BRINGING HIM BACK TO FULL HEALTH WILL DRAIN US OF ALMOST ALL OF THE ENERGON WE TOOK FROM THE DAM.
WE COULD KEEP HIM LIKE THIS AND REVIVE MORE AUTOBOT--
PRIME.
I MUST BE PART OF THIS NEW RESISTANCE.
I WANT TO FIGHT.

SHOCKWAVE. THE PORTAL BACK TO CYBERTRON HAS BEEN REPAIRED.
VERY GOOD.
BROTHER. EVEN WITH THE SPARE PARTS I HAVE GATHERED, THE WOUNDS TO RAVAGE ARE TOO DEEP. I NEED CYBERTRONIAN TECHNOLOGY. I WOULD LIKE TO TRAVEL BACK WITH YOU TO--
SOUNDWAVE! YOU MUST FOCUS ON THE TASK AT HAND!
BUT--
TAKE THIS MOMENT OF QUIET TO REFLECT ON YOUR PRIORITIES WHILE I CHECK ON THE STATUS OF MY FORTRESS!
ZHWOP
LEADER SHOCKWAVE! WHAT NEWS OF THIS NEW TREASURE TROVE?
YES! LET US SEE THE NEW WORLD THAT HAS BROUGHT OUR ENERGON RESERVES TO LEVELS HIGHER THAN THEY'VE BEEN IN CENTURIES!
AND WHAT OF OUR BROTHERS??? ONSLAUGHT AND BRAWL?!
SILENCE, DOGS!!!! DO NOT CONCERN YOURSELVES WITH SUCH MATTERS! SHOULD YOU NOT BE WATCHING THE WALLS OF THIS PLACE?
OUR ENERGON READINGS WILL BE SPIKING THE AUTOBOT REBELS' SENSORS! MAN THE BATTLEMENTS AND PREPARE FOR ASSAULT! THEY KNOW WHAT POWER WE WIELD NOW!
AND WHAT A BEAUTIFUL POWER IT IS.
"I'VE TAKEN SOME SURFACE SCANS OF THE PART OF CYBERTRON IN EARTH'S ORBIT."

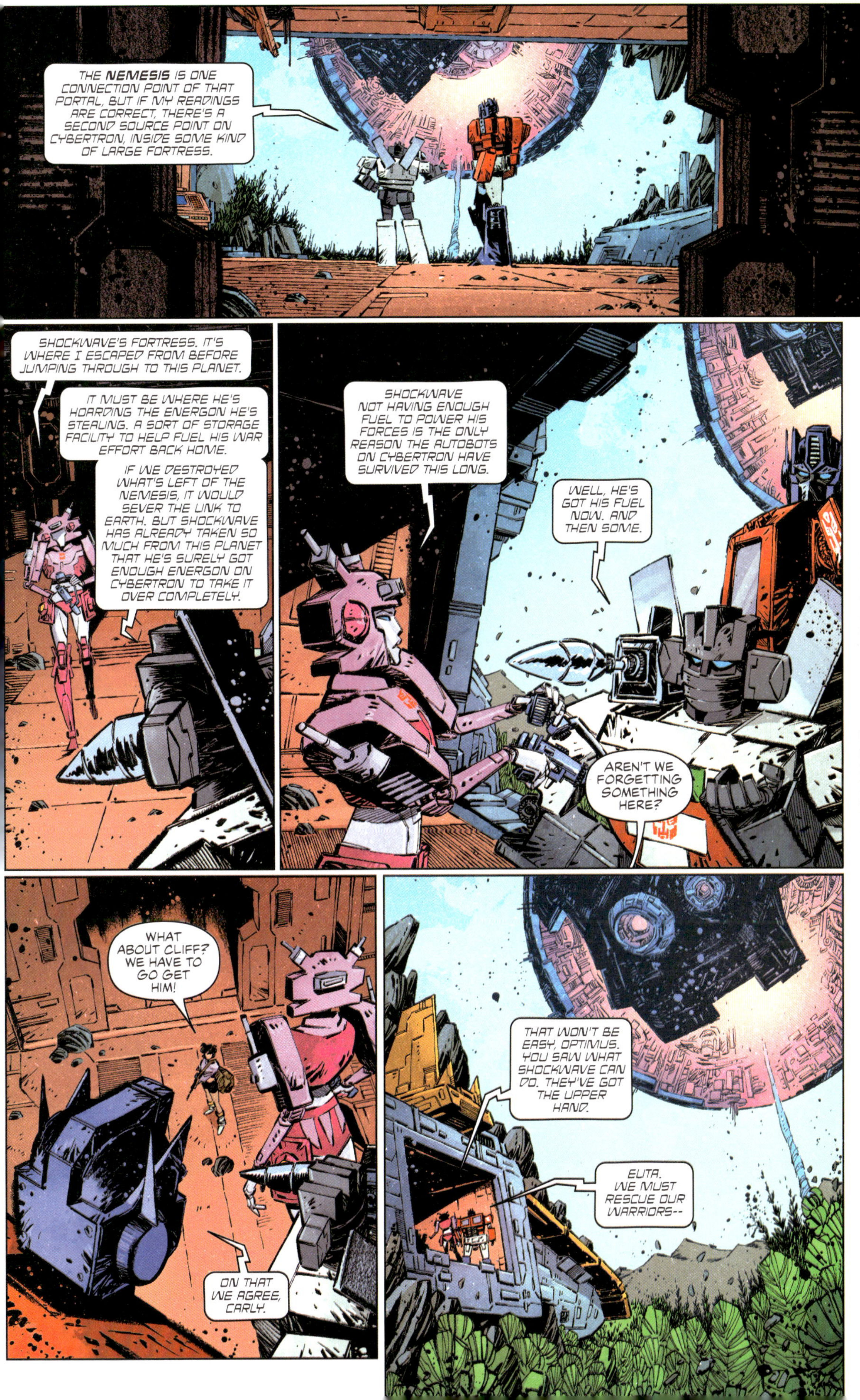

THE NEMESIS IS ONE CONNECTION POINT OF THAT PORTAL, BUT IF MY READINGS ARE CORRECT, THERE'S A SECOND SOURCE POINT ON CYBERTRON, INSIDE SOME KIND OF LARGE FORTRESS.
SHOCKWAVE'S FORTRESS. IT'S WHERE I ESCAPED FROM BEFORE JUMPING THROUGH TO THIS PLANET.
IT MUST BE WHERE HE'S HOARDING THE ENERGON HE'S STEALING. A SORT OF STORAGE FACILITY TO HELP FUEL HIS WAR EFFORT BACK HOME.
IF WE DESTROYED WHAT'S LEFT OF THE NEMESIS, IT WOULD SEVER THE LINK TO EARTH. BUT SHOCKWAVE HAS ALREADY TAKEN SO MUCH FROM THIS PLANET THAT HE'S SURELY GOT ENOUGH ENERGON ON CYBERTRON TO TAKE IT OVER COMPLETELY.
SHOCKWAVE NOT HAVING ENOUGH FUEL TO POWER HIS FORCES IS THE ONLY REASON THE AUTOBOTS ON CYBERTRON HAVE SURVIVED THIS LONG.
WELL, HE'S GOT HIS FUEL NOW. AND THEN SOME.
AREN'T WE FORGETTING SOMETHING HERE?
WHAT ABOUT CLIFF? WE HAVE TO GO GET HIM!
ON THAT WE AGREE, CARLY.
THAT WON'T BE EASY, OPTIMUS. YOU SAW WHAT SHOCKWAVE CAN DO. THEY'VE GOT THE UPPER HAND.
ELITA. WE MUST RESCUE OUR WARRIORS--

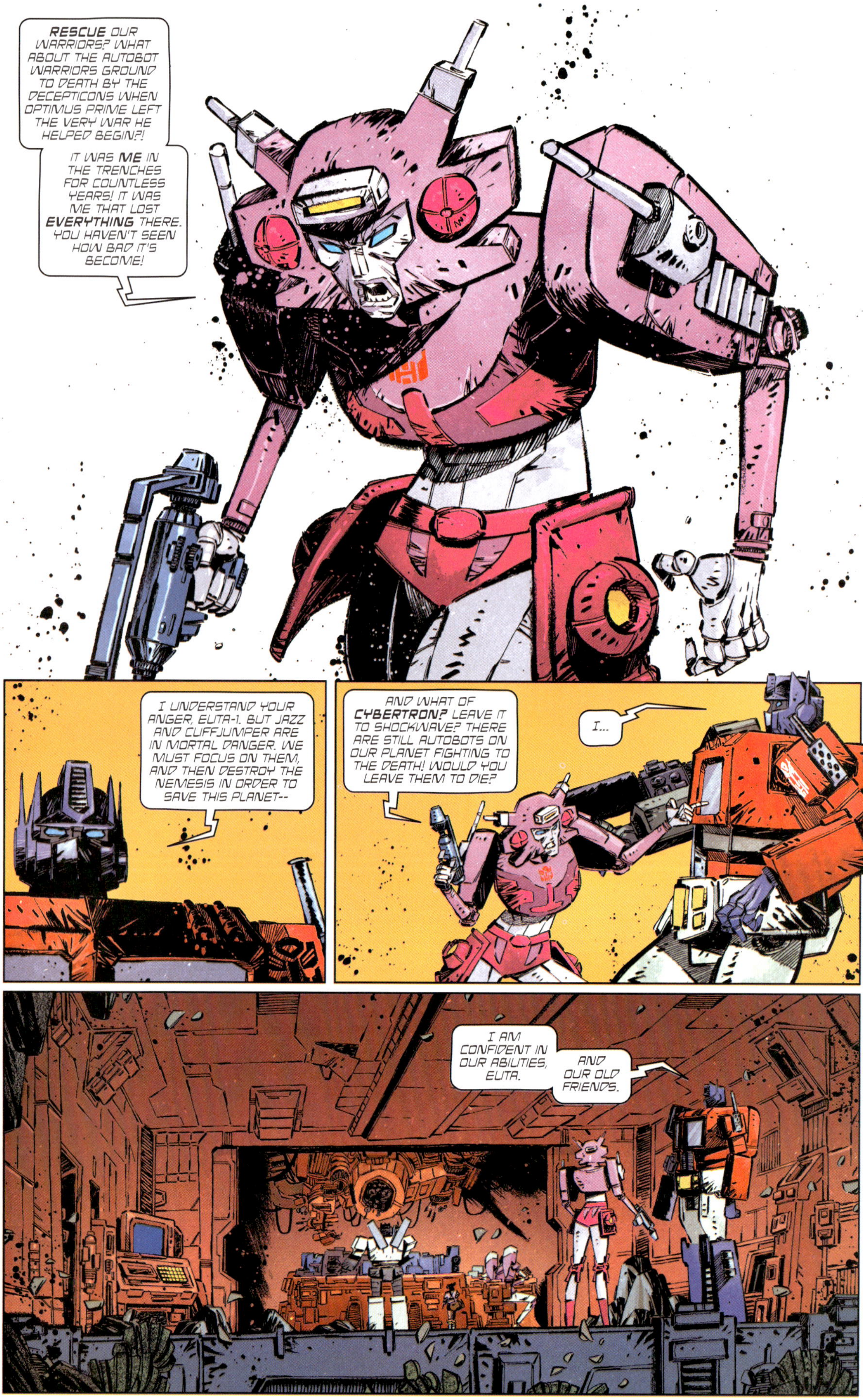
RESCUE OUR WARRIORS? WHAT ABOUT THE AUTOBOT WARRIORS GROUND TO DEATH BY THE DECEPTICONS WHEN OPTIMUS PRIME LEFT THE VERY WAR HE HELPED BEGIN?!
IT WAS ME IN THE TRENCHES FOR COUNTLESS YEARS! IT WAS ME THAT LOST EVERYTHING THERE. YOU HAVEN'T SEEN HOW BAD IT'S BECOME!
I UNDERSTAND YOUR ANGER, ELITA-1. BUT JAZZ AND CLIFFJUMPER ARE IN MORTAL DANGER. WE MUST FOCUS ON THEM, AND THEN DESTROY THE NEMESIS IN ORDER TO SAVE THIS PLANET--
AND WHAT OF CYBERTRON? LEAVE IT TO SHOCKWAVE? THERE ARE STILL AUTOBOTS ON OUR PLANET FIGHTING TO THE DEATH! WOULD YOU LEAVE THEM TO DIE?
I...
I AM CONFIDENT IN OUR ABILITIES, ELITA.
AND OUR OLD FRIENDS.

I CAN'T BELIEVE WHAT THEY DID TO MAGNIS.
KCHAK
THEY'RE ANIMALS.
THEY DON'T DESERVE TO EXIST.
UH... BUT WHAT ABOUT ALL THAT TALK ABOUT--
ARCEE.
I JUST WANTED TO--
PLEASE, ELITA. LET'S JUST FORGET IT.
JUST--LISTEN. I WAS GOING TO SAY, IT'S GOOD TO SEE A FIRE STILL INSIDE YOU.

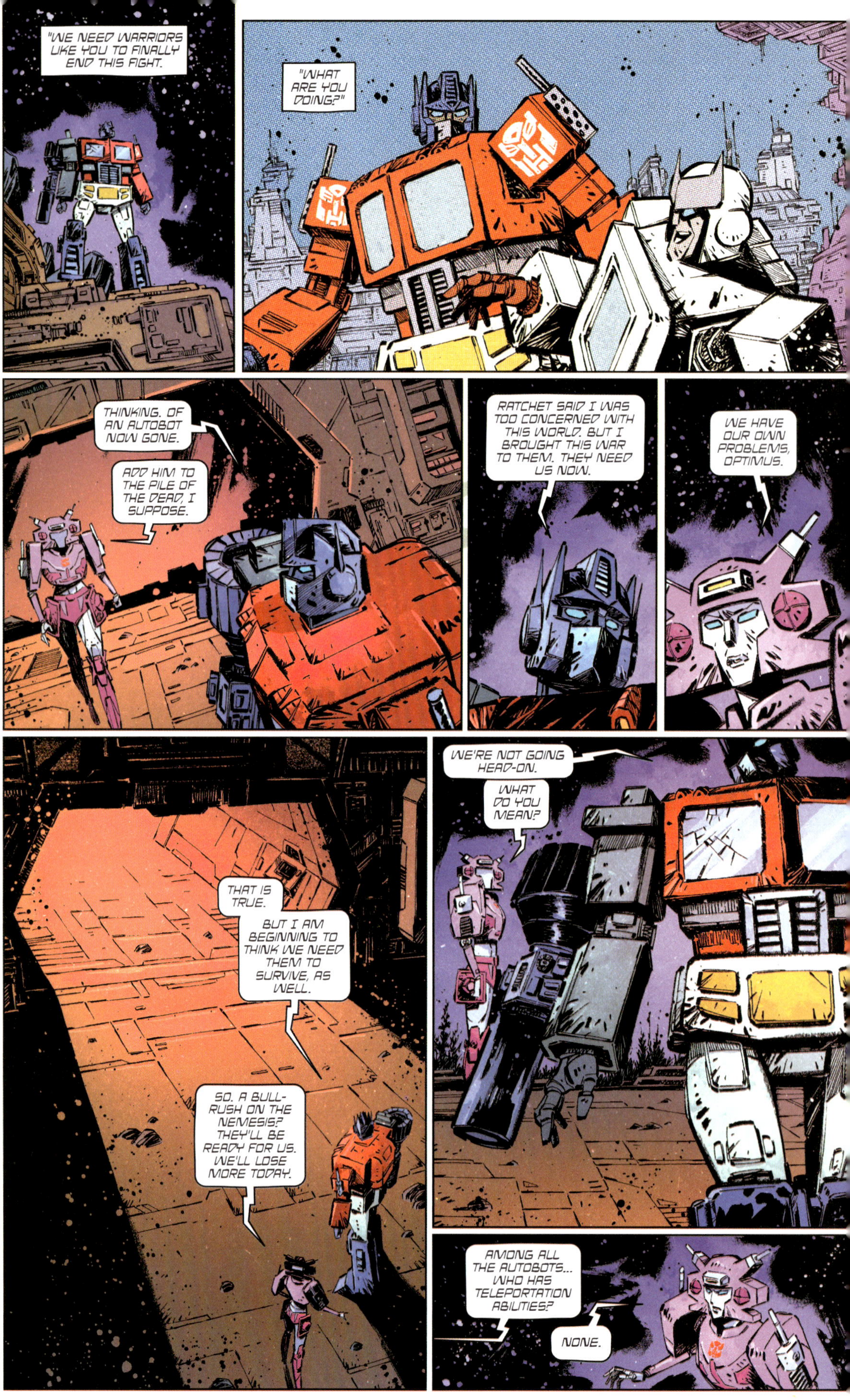
"WE NEED WARRIORS LIKE YOU TO FINALLY END THIS FIGHT.
"WHAT ARE YOU DOING?"
THINKING. OF AN AUTOBOT NOW GONE.
ADD HIM TO THE PILE OF THE DEAD, I SUPPOSE.
RATCHET SAID I WAS TOO CONCERNED WITH THIS WORLD. BUT I BROUGHT THIS WAR TO THEM. THEY NEED US NOW.
WE HAVE OUR OWN PROBLEMS, OPTIMUS.
THAT IS TRUE.
BUT I AM BEGINNING TO THINK WE NEED THEM TO SURVIVE, AS WELL.
SO. A BULL-RUSH ON THE NEMESIS? THEY'LL BE READY FOR US. WE'LL LOSE MORE TODAY.
WE'RE NOT GOING HEAD-ON.
WHAT DO YOU MEAN?
AMONG ALL THE AUTOBOTS... WHO HAS TELEPORTATION ABILITIES?
NONE.

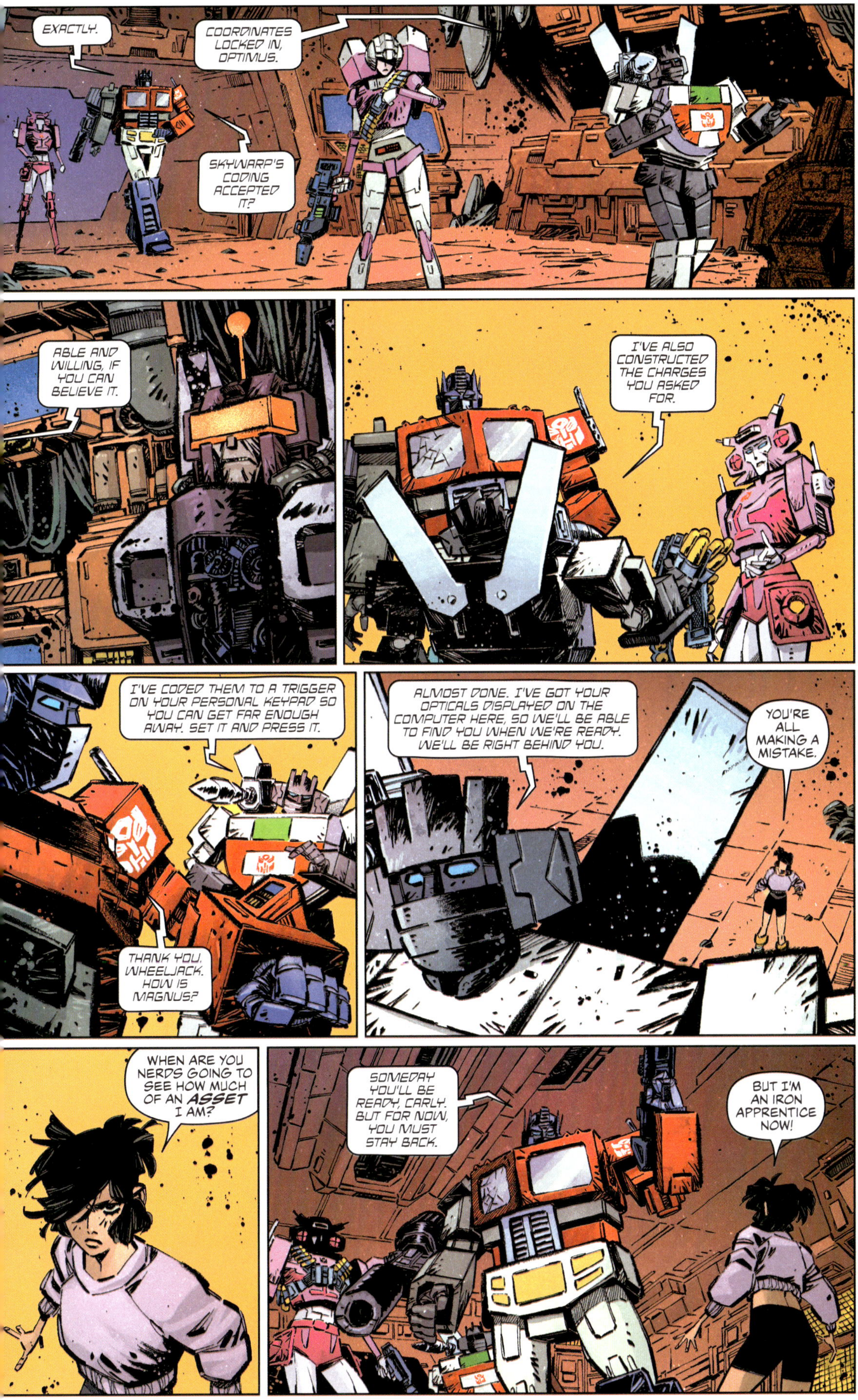
EXACTLY.
COORDINATES LOCKED IN, OPTIMUS.
SKYWARP'S CODING ACCEPTED IT?
ABLE AND WILLING, IF YOU CAN BELIEVE IT.
I'VE ALSO CONSTRUCTED THE CHARGES YOU ASKED FOR.
I'VE CODED THEM TO A TRIGGER ON YOUR PERSONAL KEYPAD SO YOU CAN GET FAR ENOUGH AWAY. SET IT AND PRESS IT.
THANK YOU, WHEELJACK. HOW IS MAGNUS?
ALMOST DONE. I'VE GOT YOUR OPTICALS DISPLAYED ON THE COMPUTER HERE, SO WE'LL BE ABLE TO FIND YOU WHEN WE'RE READY. WE'LL BE RIGHT BEHIND YOU.
YOU'RE ALL MAKING A MISTAKE.
WHEN ARE YOU NERDS GOING TO SEE HOW MUCH OF AN ASSET I AM?
SOMEDAY YOU'LL BE READY, CARLY. BUT FOR NOW, YOU MUST STAY BACK.
BUT I'M AN IRON APPRENTICE NOW!

AND I AM YOUR IRON INTERCESSOR, LIKE MAGNUS WAS FOR ME. AND I CAN'T HAVE WHAT HAPPENED TO HIM HAPPEN TO YOU.
OH, SCREW THAT! CLIFFJUMPER SAVED ME SO MANY TIMES!
I JUST GOTTA GET HIM BACK.
I WILL SAVE HIM, CARLY.
I PROMISE.

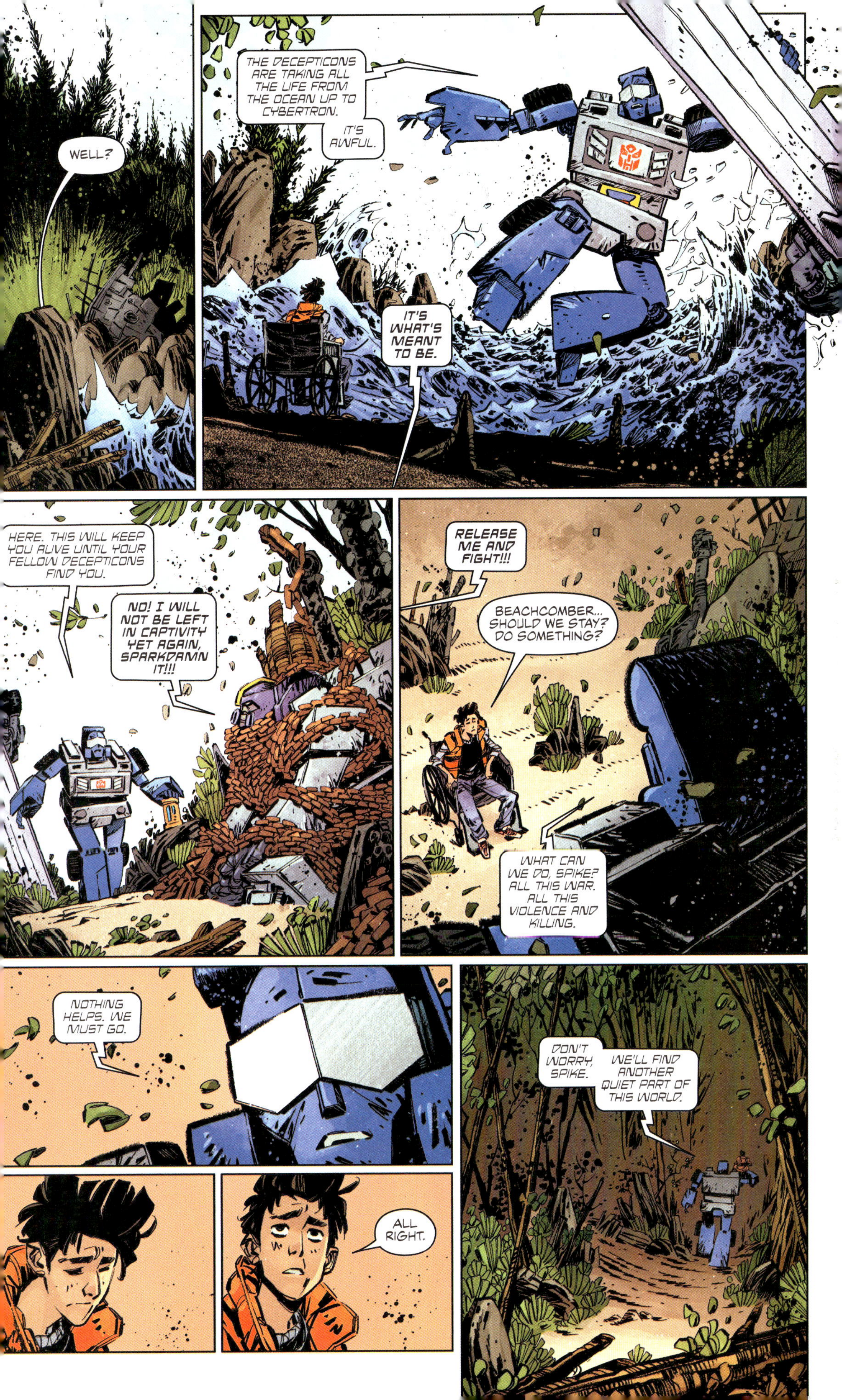
WELL?
THE DECEPTICONS ARE TAKING ALL THE LIFE FROM THE OCEAN UP TO CYBERTRON.
IT'S AWFUL.
IT'S WHAT'S MEANT TO BE.
HERE. THIS WILL KEEP YOU ALIVE UNTIL YOUR FELLOW DECEPTICONS FIND YOU.
NO! I WILL NOT BE LEFT IN CAPTIVITY YET AGAIN, SPARKDAMN IT!!!
RELEASE ME AND FIGHT!!!
BEACHCOMBER... SHOULD WE STAY? DO SOMETHING?
WHAT CAN WE DO, SPIKE? ALL THIS WAR. ALL THIS VIOLENCE AND KILLING.
NOTHING HELPS. WE MUST GO.
ALL RIGHT.
DON'T WORRY, SPIKE.
WE'LL FIND ANOTHER QUIET PART OF THIS WORLD.

I KNOW HOW YOU FEEL, BEACHCOMBER.
IT FEELS... WRONG TO FIGHT.
BUT I DON'T THINK I HAVE TO.
I JUST KNOW I CAN'T RUN AWAY.

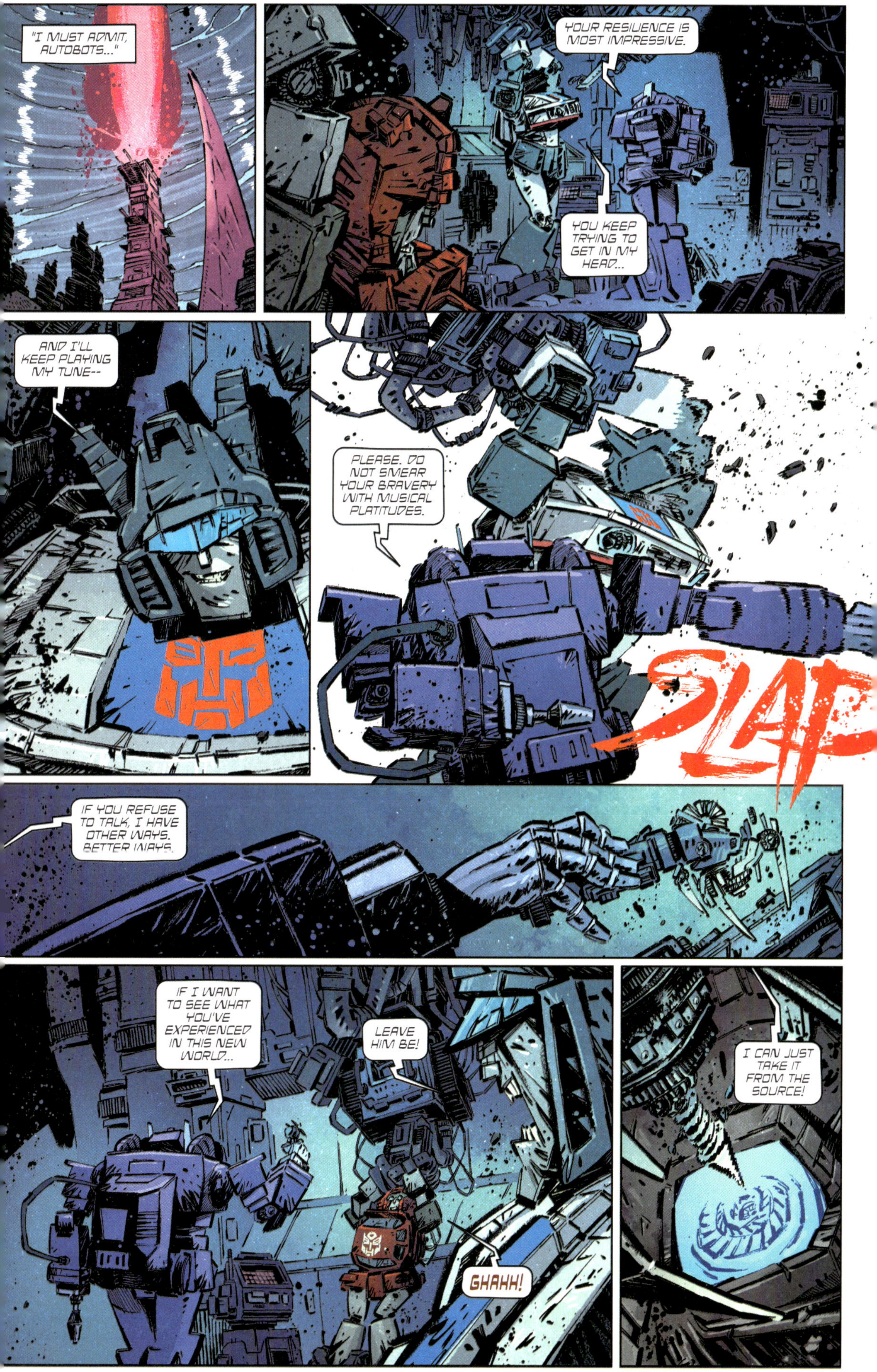
"I MUST ADMIT, AUTOBOTS..."
YOUR RESILIENCE IS MOST IMPRESSIVE.
YOU KEEP TRYING TO GET IN MY HEAD...
AND I'LL KEEP PLAYING MY TUNE--
PLEASE. DO NOT SMEAR YOUR BRAVERY WITH MUSICAL PLATITUDES.
SLAP
IF YOU REFUSE TO TALK, I HAVE OTHER WAYS. BETTER WAYS.
IF I WANT TO SEE WHAT YOU'VE EXPERIENCED IN THIS NEW WORLD...
LEAVE HIM BE!
GHAHH!
I CAN JUST TAKE IT FROM THE SOURCE!

YOU SHALL DO NO SUCH THING, DECEPTICON.
TNK
WHA--?
DROP IT.
HOW ARE YOU DOING, MY OLD FRIENDS?
I'LL BE ALL RIGHT, OPTIMUS. BUT CLIFF IS HURT BAD.
AGH--
ELITA, ARE THE CHARGES SET?
JUST PLANTED THE LAST ONE. LET'S GET THE HECK OUT OF--
HOW DOES IT FEEL, DECEPTICON?

DOES IT FEEL GOOD TO BE ON THE OTHER SIDE OF A LOADED BARREL? HOW ABOUT I END THIS RIGHT NOW?
ARCEE, STOP.
REMEMBER HOW FAR YOU'VE COME. DON'T LOSE YOURSELF TO THIS PATH AGA--
FOOLS!
GYAH!!
PEEW
PEEW
PEEW
NOT ANOTHER STEP!!!

COWARD.
ZWAP
ZWAP
ZWAP
TO ME, MY DECEPTICONS!!!
WHAT THE--?
AUTOBOTS!
COMBINE YOURSELVES, PRESENTLY!!!
INTO DEVASTATOR!!!

RAGGGHH!
SPARKDAMN IT ALL!
BOOM!!!
DON'T WORRY, ELITA.
SOUNDWAVE! WHAT IS THAT?!
SOME SORT OF PORTAL!
THIS IS WHY WE HAVE BACKUP.

AW YEAH!!!

I...
I...I...
MAGNUS?
KTONGG
CHAK CHOK CHOK
I'M SORRY-
I CAN'T--
MAGNUS, WHERE ARE YOU GOING?!
I CAN'T.
HAHAHA! I BROKE HIS MIND!
AND NOW I SHALL BREAK YOUR BODIES!

OH NO...
CLIFF!
DECEPTICONS!
LET US BE DONE WITH THIS AUTOBOT BLIGHT--
CHEE CHK
CHK CHAK
CHEE

--FOREVER!
WHAT HAPPENED TO MAGNUS??!
PEEW PEEW
PEEW
I DO NOT KNOW!
WE'RE IN THE CIRCLE PIT NOW!
CHKT
PRND21
CHAK
VRRRR
RRRRRRRR
VROOOOOO
OPTIMUS, ARE YOU STILL CONNECTED TO THE CHARGES?
ELITA SET THEM, BUT I CAN'T BLOW THE NEMESIS WITH CLIFFJUMPER SO CLOSE--
WHEN ARE YOU ALL GONNA LEARN??

I'M HERE TO STAY!
WHAT--
AND I'M HERE TO FIGHT!!!
SLAMMM
KCHOM
KCHOM
KCHOM
...CARLY?
HEY, BUDDY.
I'M SORRY FOR NOT BEING THERE FOR YOU S--

SKUISHHH
GYAH!!!
AUTOBOTS! WHILE THEY'RE DISTRACTED! LET'S GET OUR FALLEN BROTHER!
CHARGE!!!
KAH
HURRY! GET OUT--
SKREEUNK
TOSS!
NO!
MY ARM! IT'S-- STUCK--!

AUTOBOT BRAT!!!
KICK
YEOW!
CLIFFJUMPER!
COMBATICONS! LET'S GET INTO THE AC--
SHWOMMM
BOOMMM

HAHA!
NOW, ELITA!
POOM
VRRRRR
K-CHINK!
VWA VWA VWA
NO--
RRRRRRR

SHKRAKKITHOOOM
MY HARVESTER!! NOOO!
VRWOMMMM
OPTIMUS! UNLESS MY READINGS ARE MISTAKEN--
"CYBERTRON IS BEGINNING TO GO BACK THROUGH THE PORTAL!"
"BUT THE BEAM FROM THE NEMESIS IS STILL ACTIVE!"
THAT DEVICE MUST HAVE BEEN KEEPING CYBERTRON IN PLACE AS WELL AS HARVESTING ENERGON. WITH IT GONE, OUR HOME IS SLOWLY RETURNING TO ITS PLACE IN THE GALAXY!
I SHALL BRING REINFORCEMENTS! YOU WILL SEE! YOU WILL PAY!

CLIFF! HE--
I SAW, CARLY!
OPTIMUS--THE CHARGES! WE COULD SEND CYBERTRON BACK COMPLETELY, RIGHT NOW!
BUT--
AND I WILL, WHEELJACK. BUT IT WAS ME THAT LEFT JAZZ AND CLIFFJUMPER BEHIND.
I WILL NOT LEAVE HIM AGAIN!
THEN DO AWAY WITH THIS PEST, AND LET'S GET BACK TO BUS--
UH, GUYS...
OH, SH--

HE'S TOO STRONG!
RETREAT!!!
COWARDS! STAND AND FIGHT!!!
COME ON, THEN.

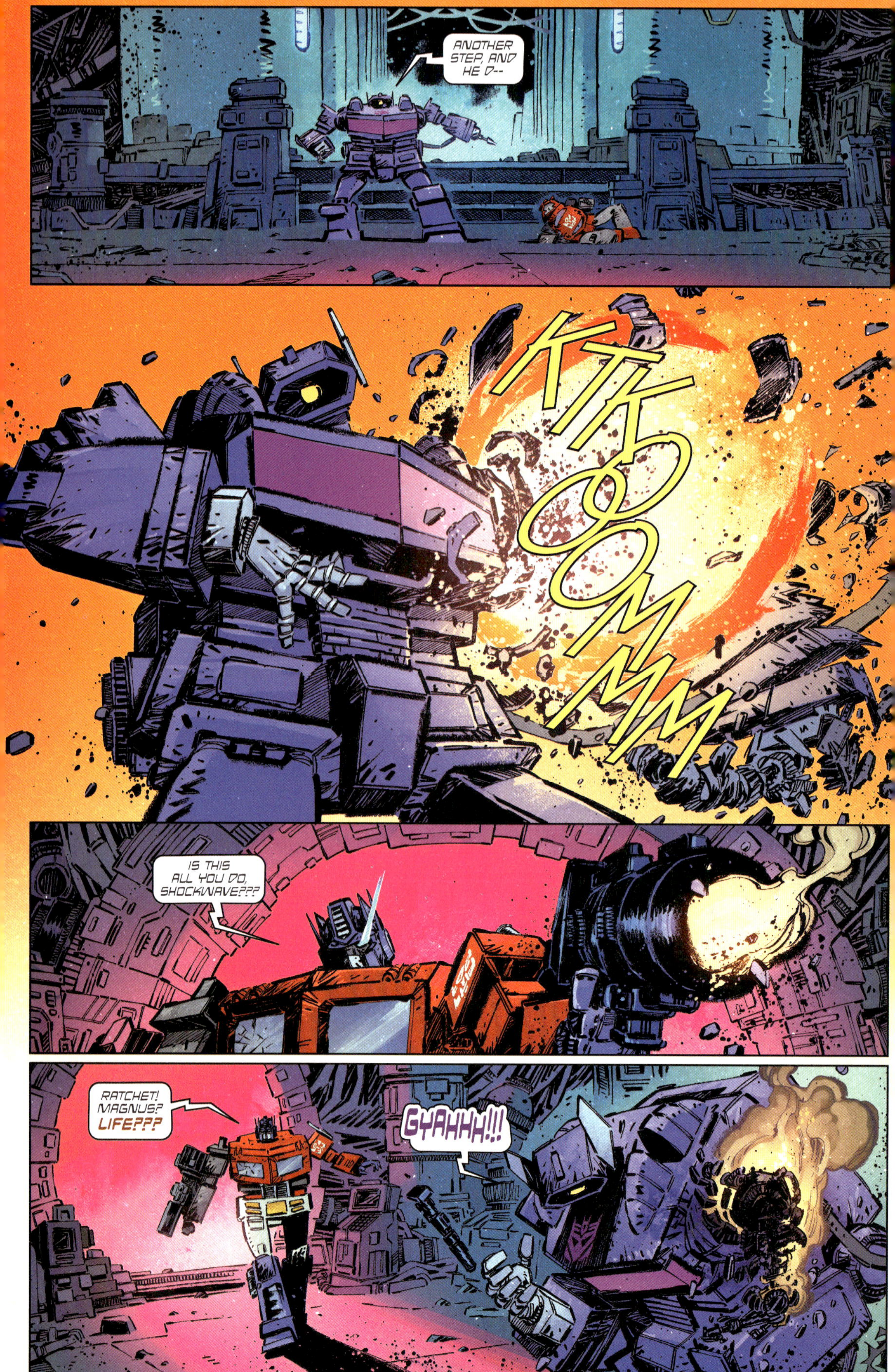
ANOTHER STEP, AND HE D--
KTKOOOMMM
IS THIS ALL YOU DO, SHOCKWAVE???
RATCHET! MAGNUS? LIFE???
GYAHHH!!!

ALL YOU DO IS TAKE AWAY WHAT IS GOOD!
BOOM
BOOM
BOOM
BOOM
BOOM
GYAH!!!
BRAAAAAA
GAHHH!!!
G-GKKKK--
KKKK--
KRAK

I...
OPTIMUS?
WHAT... HAVE I DONE...?
WELCOME BACK TO THE WAR, OPTIMUS PRIME.
I FINALLY SEE YOUR OLD SELF RETURNING.
NO...I'M NOT LIKE THAT ANYMORE, ELITA. I...SOMETHING CAME OVER ME. I DON'T KNOW WHAT IT WAS.

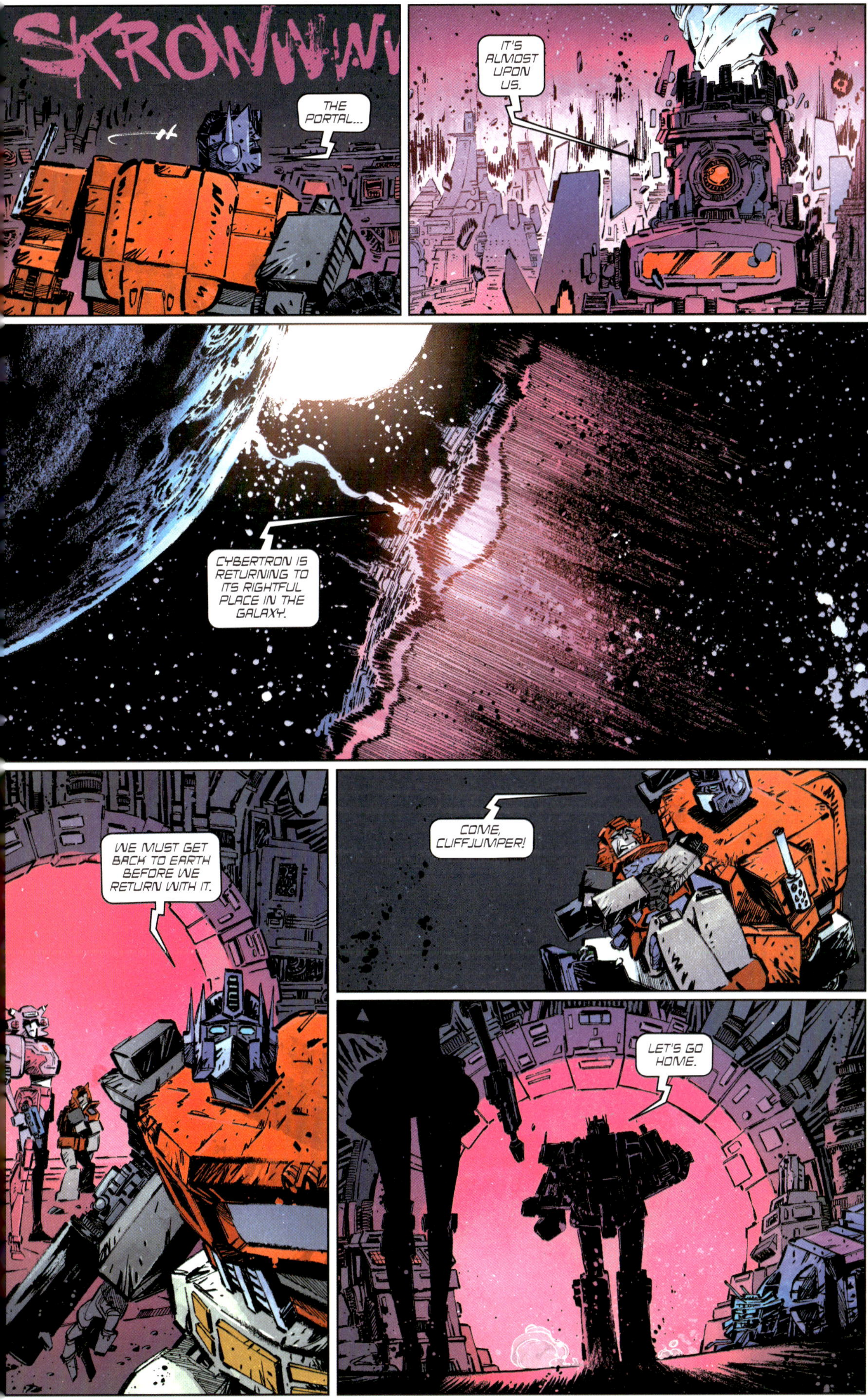
SKROWWW
THE PORTAL...
IT'S ALMOST UPON US.
CYBERTRON IS RETURNING TO ITS RIGHTFUL PLACE IN THE GALAXY.
WE MUST GET BACK TO EARTH BEFORE WE RETURN WITH IT.
COME, CLIFFJUMPER!
LET'S GO HOME.

K-KOOM
YOU ARE HOME, OPTIMUS.
ELITA-- WHAT--?!
ELITA--
WE NEED YOU HERE. THE AUTOBOT RESISTANCE NEEDS YOU. HERE.
CLIFF?
ALL THIS ENERGON TAKEN... WE CAN USE IT. TOGETHER.

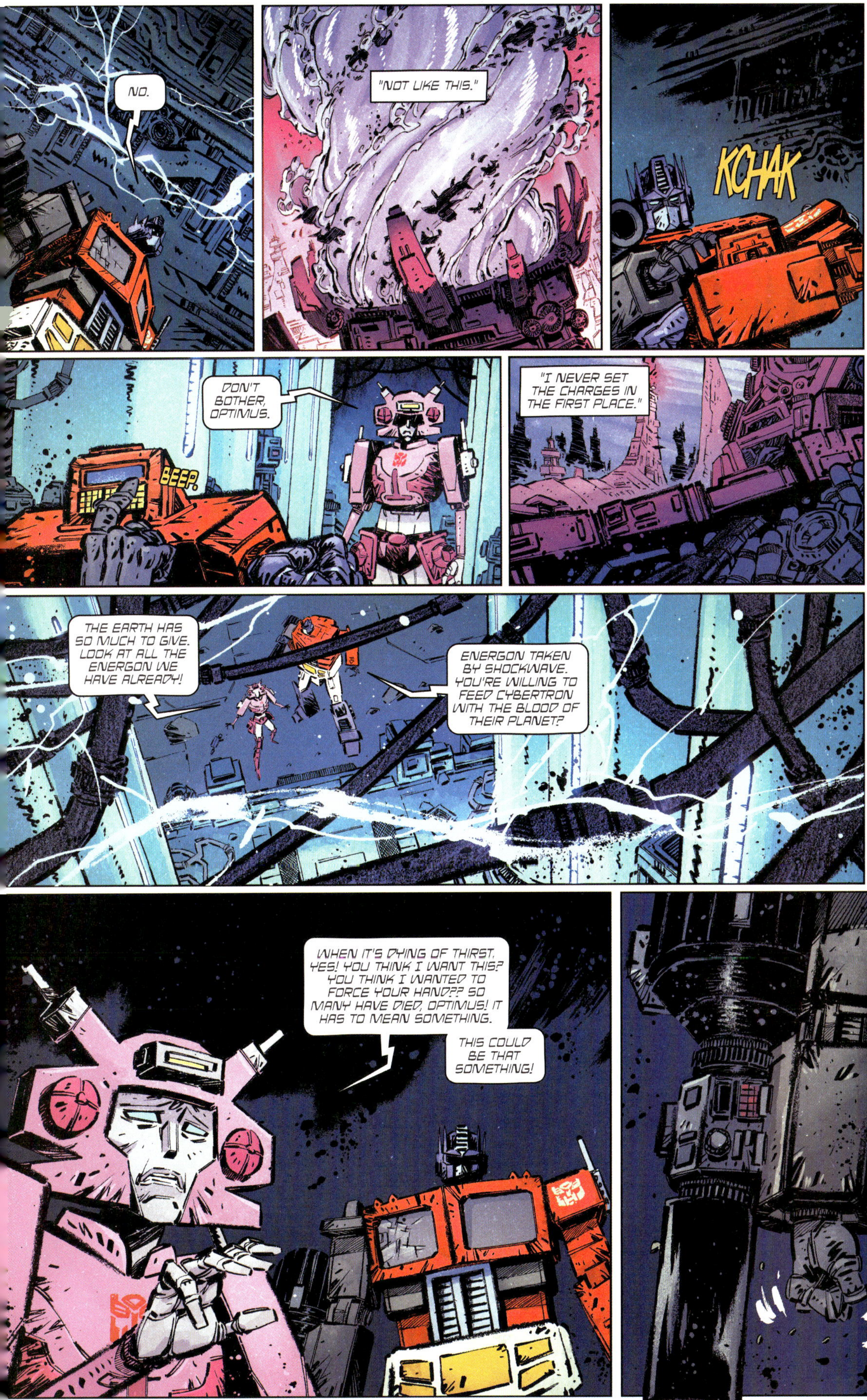
NO.
"NOT LIKE THIS."
KCHAK
DON'T BOTHER, OPTIMUS.
BEEP
"I NEVER SET THE CHARGES IN THE FIRST PLACE."
THE EARTH HAS SO MUCH TO GIVE. LOOK AT ALL THE ENERGON WE HAVE ALREADY!
ENERGON TAKEN BY SHOCKWAVE. YOU'RE WILLING TO FEED CYBERTRON WITH THE BLOOD OF THEIR PLANET?
WHEN IT'S DYING OF THIRST. YES! YOU THINK I WANT THIS? YOU THINK I WANTED TO FORCE YOUR HAND?? SO MANY HAVE DIED, OPTIMUS! IT HAS TO MEAN SOMETHING.
THIS COULD BE THAT SOMETHING!

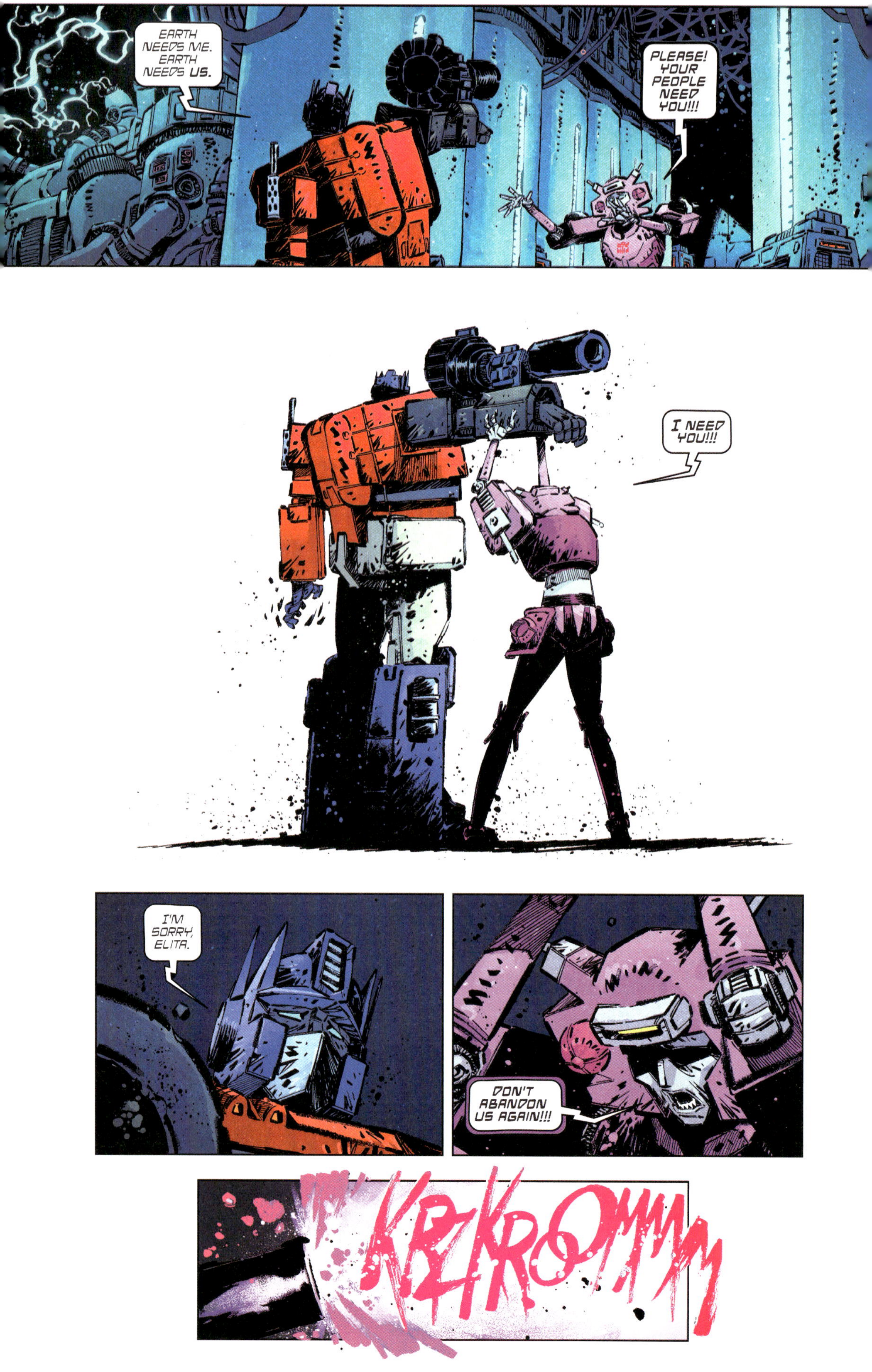
EARTH NEEDS ME. EARTH NEEDS US.
PLEASE! YOUR PEOPLE NEED YOU!!!
I NEED YOU!!!
I'M SORRY, ELITA.
DON'T ABANDON US AGAIN!!!
KRKROOMMM

SHKKKKKKKKK
GAH...
YOU CHOSE.

YOU CHOSE EARTH OVER US.

SSSSSSSS
SSSSSSSSS
AGHH--IT-BURNS--
IF THIS...
IS THE END OF MY SPARK...
THEN I THANK THE PRIMES THAT THIS WILL BE MY LAST SIGHT.
I KNOW, OPTIMUS.

THIS PLACE REVEALS NEW BEAUTIES EVERY MOMENT.
BEACH... COMBER...?

WHAT HAVE I DONE?

WHAT HAVE I DONE?

VOLUME

02

/ END /